MW00873736

TEN $1 BILLS

THE AMAZING TRUE STORY OF HOW GOD BLESSED TEN ONE-DOLLAR BILLS AND BUILT A BRIDGE IN NICARAGUA

THOMAS BLACK

WESTBOW
PRESS
A DIVISION OF THOMAS NELSON

WestBow Press books may be ordered through booksellers or by contacting:

WestBow Press
A Division of Thomas Nelson
1663 Liberty Drive
Bloomington, IN 47403
www.westbowpress.com
1-(866) 928-1240

ISBN: 978-1-4497-6103-5 (sc)

Library of Congress Control Number: 2012913531

Printed in the United States of America

WestBow Press rev. date: 07/31/2012

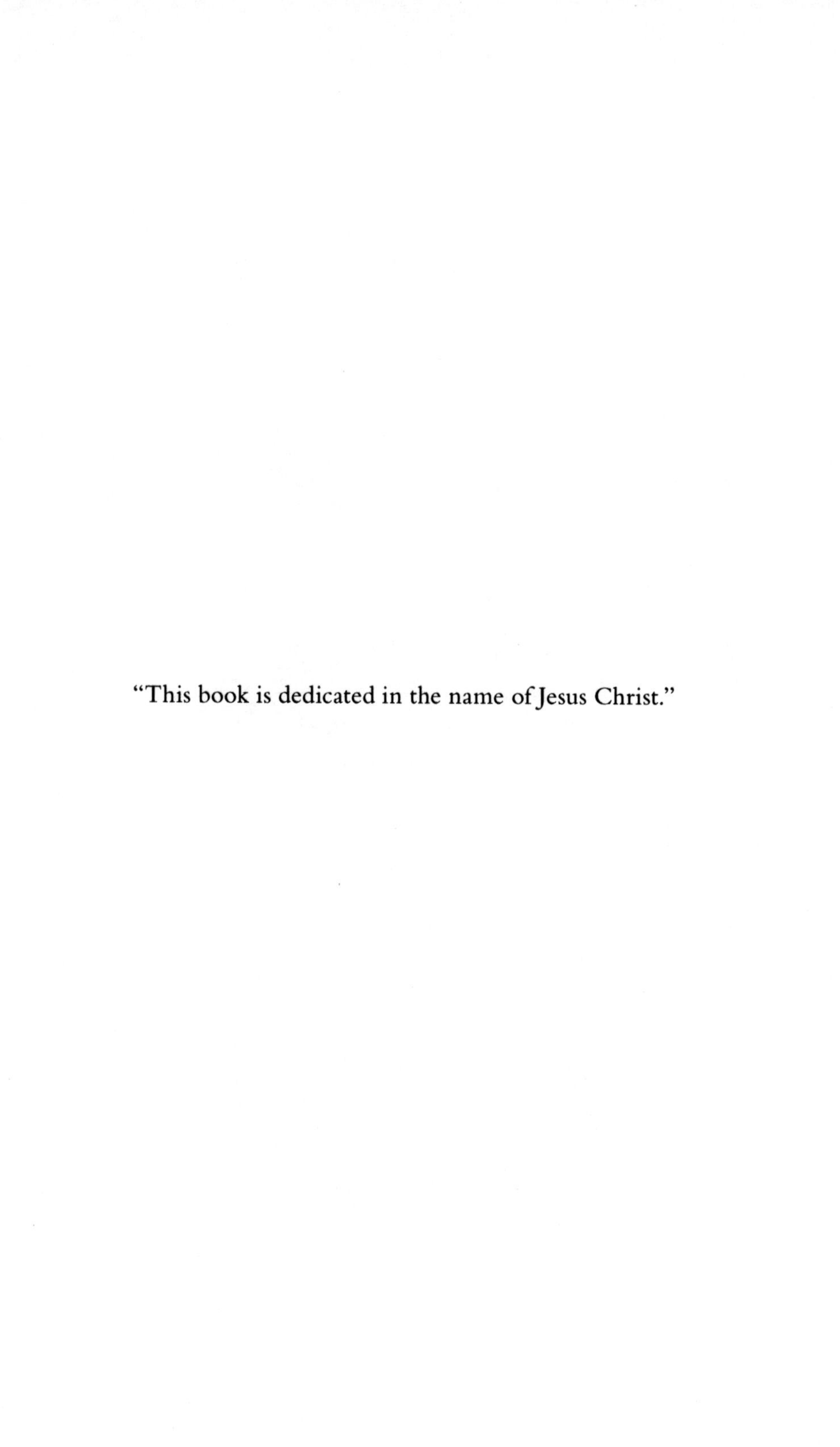

"This book is dedicated in the name of Jesus Christ."

This book is written
in memory of my mother,
Juanita Gardner Black
(1934-1989)

". . . we should love people not only with words and talk, but by our actions and true caring."

1 John 3:18 NCV

CONTENTS

FOREWORD

If bees can keep our entire world in bloom, then we can just as easily spread God's grace to His "forgotten" poor in distant lands. Thomas is not only that bee, but one who shares his grace with others in seemingly infinite amounts. There but for the grace of God he goes building bridges, not only to help others cross, but to demonstrate the power of the Cross.

—Kenneth R. Frantz
Volunteer and Founder
Bridges to Prosperity, Inc.*

*About Bridges to Prosperity—Bridges to Prosperity connects isolated rural communities around the world with services found on the other side of raging rivers by building footbridges. A registered 501(c)(3) non-profit organization, Bridges to Prosperity has no religious affiliation and the perspectives expressed in this book are the author's alone.

INTRODUCTION

The Bridge

It was one Sunday in January of 2010 when Mike talked with me after the church worship service, asking if I had found a bridge design. I carefully worded my reply to him, "Yes, I printed two bridge design manuals off my computer last week, and have a friend who has agreed to help with the foundation designs. We need to schedule a trip to the proposed bridge site so we can take measurements, perform a survey, and take soil samples." Still recovering from back surgery and the expenses associated with it, Mike suggested we wait until April. I felt an immediate sigh of relief when he spoke those words.

As a project engineer, I had successfully managed the construction of several electrical substations, including the design and steel details, but this pedestrian bridge project in Nicaragua was beginning to overwhelm me. Even though I had read through those design manuals several times, I was an electrical engineer, not a civil engineer. Plus, managing a project of this magnitude from the States seemed nearly impossible to me. At this point, I really had doubts about the project's success. And my repeated requests for help, for someone more qualified to go with me to Nicaragua, if only to assist in the site evaluation, only fell upon deaf ears.

But if not me, who would be "called" to build this community a footbridge? "A bridge," as Mike had explained at the Nicaragua Mission Team meeting in December of 2008, "is needed by the Gavilan and Patastule communities during the rainy months of May, June, July, August and September, during which time the Bulbul River becomes impassable. This means the villagers must travel at least two hours to an alternate crossing location, which during the days of heavy rains can itself become impassable."

He retold a story, "A whole family was crossing the Bulbul River in a small truck. There had been a rain storm further up in the mountains.

Suddenly a wall of water came down the canyon and caught them in the middle of the river. The truck was swept away, turning over several times in the river. The people who saw it happen tried to save them, but there was no hope. The whole family drowned."

Mike continued, "The bridge would benefit the school teacher who must cross the river to teach the community children, the farmer who must carry his fresh milk across to sell in the nearby town, the mother who must cross to get needed supplies for her family, and the sick person who needs to cross to receive medical attention. They don't need us to change their lifestyle, only provide them with a bridge."

For these reasons, and because I have a passion for helping other people, the bridge project really struck my interest. But the only commitment I had made during that team meeting was simply to find out more information, and I had done that. Then the thought occurred to me, *Maybe I should just give Mike the design manuals so my part would be done.* But as I drove home that Sunday, I remembered how I came upon those two manuals while searching the Internet.

After the mission team meeting that December, I had spent the following month e-mailing friends at the Department of Transportation and also a few civil engineers, simply asking if they would help in designing the footbridge. Months went by without a single response. I did receive several pictures of covered wooden bridges and a few pedestrian bridges, but they all looked too expensive and very difficult to build in a developing country like Nicaragua.

At that point, I decided to start searching the Internet. I sat for what seemed like hours typing combination of words: *bridges, bridge design manuals, designing bridges, pedestrian bridges*, etc. Three of the Internet searches yielded practically the same results, with the first couple of pages filled with articles on famous traffic bridges, then the remaining search pages filled with fun topics such as "How to Play Bridge." The last search provided a page filled with pictures of rope bridges, but nothing on how to design a pedestrian footbridge to modern standards. I was discouraged, to say the least.

Then late the next night after further searching still yielded no fruitful results, I typed one last time: *pedestrian bridge design manual.* At that moment, I closed my eyes and softly whispered, "Lord, I need Your help. I need You to show me a bridge design manual." As a Christian, I was used to praying for individuals who were sick and for families who had lost a loved one—but not for simple, everyday things.

Quickly glancing over the first page and then over to page two, I saw most of the same search results as before. Then suddenly, I heard His voice, "Go to page eleven." I admit I doubted a little, because I already knew that none of the articles past page three were about footbridges. But going on nothing but faith, I clicked on page eleven. There, at the top of page eleven, were the words "How to Design Suspended Bridges," and just beneath it, "How to Design Suspension Bridges." I was simply amazed as I smiled towards the ceiling. *Now . . . who would believe this?* I wondered. Well, it didn't really matter, because I had found, or He had shown me, what I needed to get started.

I spent the remainder of 2009 reading through those bridge design manuals, studying the math, and trying to get a grip on the scope of the project. The logistics were enormous, but one fact stuck out in all of the design documentation: "You must know the soil conditions so the foundations can be properly designed." That seemed to be step one.

But even after Mike and I talked that Sunday, I was still apprehensive about building the bridge. So many questions remained unanswered in my mind, with the most important being, "How can I make sure this project is going to be successful?" In the mission team meeting that December, someone had mentioned putting a bridge plaque on the bridge which would read, "This bridge is dedicated in the name of Jesus Christ." To me, that was a bold statement. And from that moment, I knew if His name was going be on it, then it *had* to be done right.

CHAPTER ONE

TURNING IT ALL OVER TO GOD

It was now March of 2010, and I was worried. Over a year of searching for help, sending out e-mails and making phone calls; nevertheless, they all appeared to be dead-ends. Though one friend had now agreed to help in designing the bridge's foundations, that was only step one. Step two was actually going to Nicaragua and doing a survey at the bridge site, analyzing the soil conditions, and then producing detailed drawings so a material cost estimate could be prepared. The material cost estimate was so my church and the town of Matiguas would know the financial commitment it would take to build the bridge.

Then an important point popped in my mind—I was an electrical engineer . . . not a civil engineer. Being a registered Professional Engineer, I knew what the Code of Ethics for Professional Engineers said about practicing engineering outside of one's "field of expertise," meaning if the bridge fell, I could lose my license . . . but even worse than that, I could be sued by the Nicaraguan government. There appeared to be a lot of risks associated with the project for not only me personally, but also my church.

And several questions remained. Questions like, "Who would supervise the building of the bridge? To what standard of construction, and to what strength of concrete?" I was out of answers. The enormity of this project had finally started to sink in: all the issues, all the logistics, and all the unknowns. Maybe this is why no one had come forward to help . . . maybe this project *was* too big. To tell someone we wanted to build a 250 foot pedestrian walking bridge across a raging river in Nicaragua did sound crazy.

Where was my faith in my God, you might ask, *a God who could fit this bridge project in the palm of his hand?* To me, this was not yet a faith project, but merely a physical bridge with physical engineering design problems. And besides, what other door was there for me to knock on? As an engineer, I had done everything humanly possible to tap into engineering resources, but still nothing. Only wasted time waiting for answers that never came and watching doors that never opened. It now seemed for once in my life I had taken on a project that I simply could not find a solution for. This project needed a big engineering firm to get involved, someone with a lot of expertise and a proven track record. At this point, I had exhausted all of my personal resources, so where were the answers? Prayers had been offered, but still no answers.

But then, on Monday, March 8th, I received an e-mail from Douglas. He had heard about the bridge project last year from my neighbor, Robert. I remembered him sending me pictures and information for a few bridges he saw while on vacation last year. I had even contacted one of the engineering firms who had constructed one of those bridges which looked like something that could be built in Nicaragua. But like all the others, that door never opened, either. So I was really shocked that after an entire year, he would still remember my church's bridge project.

In his e-mail, Douglas explained opening the state newspaper's Sunday edition and seeing a story in the *Parade* magazine, a small insert included in the Sunday newspaper each week. After reading the story, he remembered my church's bridge project. He didn't know the status of our project, but felt led to scan the story and e-mail it to me. As I opened the attachment to print it, the title of the story immediately caught my eye, "Building Bridges of Hope—moved by a plight away, one man takes action." As I read those words, I began to ponder, *Maybe God has a plan for this bridge after all.*

The story was about a man named Ken Frantz and Bridges to Prosperity, a non-profit organization he founded in 2001, and their work building pedestrian footbridges in developing countries. The story listed some of the existing countries where Bridges to Prosperity had built bridges, which included Ethiopia, Nepal, Indonesia and South America, but NOT Nicaragua. I read a little bit more before tossing it to the side on my desk. I thought to myself, *Here's someone building bridges exactly like the one we need to build in Nicaragua, but how would I convince them to help my church with our bridge? And besides, why would they be any different than the others I had already tried to contact?*

That story sat on my desk till Friday. When I went to throw it away, somehow one word caught my eye . . . *Nicaragua.* What, how did I miss that before? Further down in the article it plainly stated they were looking to build bridges in Nicaragua! Chills covered my body as I started at the beginning and read the entire article. Over a year of looking for an open door and now, could this be it . . . an article in a magazine? With all the e-mails sent to engineers and universities and now, to finally get an answer to my prayer in an e-mailed story. I got very excited about this possibility, but then reality began to sink in. We all know the old saying, "If something is too good to be true, then it probably is." And for me, a person who easily gets overly optimistic, it usually is. Why would a world-known company like Bridges to Prosperity stop to help a small country church in Blythewood, South Carolina, build a bridge in Nicaragua?

I spent that Saturday helping my wife clean the house. After taking a much-needed break, I pulled out the "Building Bridges of Hope" story from my folder and re-read it, just to see if their website was given. To my surprise, it wasn't. But after reviewing the printed e-mail, Douglas had included the Bridges to Prosperity website address. Hoping for good results, I typed in "www.BridgestoProsperity.org." This appeared to be their official company website. It was well laid out, even with a "Contact Us" pull down tab. The contact name listed was for Avery, and her e-mail address was included. *Well,* I thought, *it's at least a door.* So I knocked.

That night I typed at the computer for several hours what would soon become a four page dissertation.

March 13, 2010

Dear Avery,

Let me start off by saying that in life, finding people to dedicate their time, much less their career, to helping other people is rare. It appears you and Ken Frantz are two such people, and I commend you for that. I was really moved by the recent article in Parade *titled "Building Bridges of Hope," which is the reason I have contacted you. Let me first give you some background of my church's involvement in Nicaragua.*

Sandy Level Baptist Church in Blythewood, South Carolina, has a long, embedded history in mission work. Each year for over 12 years, my church helped individual mission teams go to Nicaragua. My church, along with other congregations, has built a feeding center and several other buildings to help the poorest of poor in several communities in Nicaragua, such as those near Matagalpa, due north from Managua. Church members Mike and Butch generally serve as project leaders, organizing materials and labor well in advance of each trip. I have never personally been, but I always enjoyed the local mission trips I would participate in during spring break while a student at Clemson University. I share a strong passion for helping other people.

In 2008, Mike received word from his friend in Nicaragua that a much needed mission project was to construct a walking bridge across a river. During the rainy season, the mountain river floods (naturally, I know) to the point it is not safe to cross, which cuts off a village of people and farmers from the mainland. To get supplies or to sell their milk, they risk their lives by forming a line while holding hands (men, women, and even children) to pass supplies across. Mr. Frantz in the Parade *article recalls witnessing a similar situation. During such a time a wall of water suddenly rushed down on them, and a whole family was tragically swept away. Several other individuals have also drowned while attempting to cross the river.*

In December of 2008, the Nicaragua Mission Team met and discussed plans for the bridge. Mike presented his idea for the bridge and what details he could remember about each proposed foundation location, and the distance, which is approximately 250 feet. As I listened and processed this information, I began to ask questions, and soon realized that no actual engineering analysis had been done to ensure the bridge would be safe; factors such as wind, adequate width to prevent twisting, cable tensions, total calculated weight of the bridge with people on it, moments of inertia on the foundations, sway, etc. But as they say, those that speak get volunteered, and I was appointed the job to do the math and design. Now, as an electrical engineer, just because I know these terms and understand them, doesn't mean I can apply the engineering principles correctly the first time without failure—which would mean wasted resources of labor and materials.

My experience: As an electrical engineer for an electric distribution cooperative, I have overseen the design of five electrical distribution substations, which all involve wire tensions and moments on steel structures. I am familiar with spread-footer foundations as well as drilled pier foundations for these structures, and the application of each. However, building a substation you do from the ground up, but a rope/wire bridge is suspended above a river (or dry land), which introduces construction techniques above my level of expertise. If it were a dry gorge crossing, a simpler way would be to construct the bridge on the ground then hoist it into place, but with a river, this may prove too difficult to accomplish.

We need a team of experts who can show us the tried and proven methods of construction.

In March of 2009, I contacted several friends at the Department of Transportation (DOT) to see if anyone there had ever designed such a project; no one had. However, I did learn that one of the coaches in my son's basketball league was a supervisor over the highway department's bridge foundation design team, and also supervised the foundation work at the new Cooper River Bridge in Charleston here in South Carolina. We have since talked and he is confident he can design the foundations, given enough information about the soil conditions and available construction area, in case a spread-footer needs to be employed (if the soil is too rocky to adequately excavate).

Also in March of 2009, I searched the Internet for suspended cable bridges and suspension bridges and found what I feel to be an excellent resource entitled "Short Span Trail Bridge Standard—Suspended Type: Volume 1: Guidelines for Survey, Design & Construction" and "Short Span Trail Bridge Standard—Suspension Type: Volume 1: Guidelines for Survey, Design & Construction." I have thoroughly reviewed both of these documents, and feel that the Suspended type is a much simpler design to construct. I have included them for your review, to see if they are good documents to follow, and provide any comments on these documents.

Now, you may be asking, a year has gone by with no progress on the bridge. Even though I have been put in charge of the design, material and construction portion of the bridge, Mike and Butch are still the organizers of the trip, which did include a medical unit and vacation Bible school leader. Unfortunately, last year Mike had to undergo back surgery for his discs and Butch had to have heart bypass surgery, so the trip was postponed until 2010, which puts us to where we are today.

We were planning to leave this Friday for Nicaragua, and fly into Managua. During this trip, we were to re-evaluate both sides of the river crossing, take additional measurements, and perform soil excavations for classification. But with already limited resources, Mike decided this week to postpone the trip until after Easter, to hopefully get better airline fares. In the mean time, someone who remembered the project sent me the article from Parade, *which had a link to the Bridges to Prosperity website.*

The website says you are out of the country until the end of April in Guatemala.

Avery, I realize this is short notice and may seem awkward to ask, but I would be so honored to meet you and learn more about the organization you work for during my trip in April. And I would be even more grateful (and appreciative like you couldn't imagine) if you could go to the site of the proposed bridge crossing with me, and either give our team of volunteers advice, or take it on as one of the "Building Bridges of Hope" projects for Nicaragua this year. That would be awesome, and I would give you and your organization two weeks of my vacation time in the summer to help with the construction of this bridge, I promise you that! I don't mind using a shovel or getting wet, and am a great problem solver. Also, there are villagers who are more than eager to help with the foundation work and construction of the bridge, which is one of your group's requirements.

In closing, I only ask that you and your organization strongly consider helping my church's Nicaragua Mission Team take this bridge from the planning stages to reality. Don't take this the wrong way, but the need is so great for this bridge that we will build it anyways, and hopefully be successful the first time. But having a knowledgeable engineer, such as you, to talk to would give me greater confidence in not only the design but the construction. If you decline, then any advice or construction tips you can share or forward, including construction pictures, would be much appreciated.

Thank you for your time,
Thomas S. Black, Jr. P.E.

cc frantzk

After I had finished typing, I sat back and carefully read back over it, making sure I hadn't made any spelling or grammatical errors—at least none that would have been apparent to an engineer. Since I didn't have an e-mail account set up on my home computer, I saved the letter on a thumb drive and drove to my office. Even though it was 9:30 p.m. on a Saturday night, this was the most important letter I had ever written.

As I lay in bed that night, the question of *What would these people think about my letter?* raced through my mind, but most importantly, *Would they respond?* This was probably the best opportunity I had come across in over a year for turning the bridge project into a reality, but most importantly, for it to be successful. I felt a small sense of hope, knowing this might be the one open door I had been praying for.

The next day at church seemed to be business as usual—Sunday school, choir, and then Pastor Ben's sermon. As Pastor Ben began the time of invitation, my mind drifted to thoughts of Avery or Ken opening the e-mail I had sent to them the night before. Would they respond to an e-mail sent by a complete stranger, or even worse, were they such a big company that my e-mail would be lost among the hundreds of others they must receive each day?

I knew I had done all I could, putting forth my best effort. I reflected back on all I had done—all my efforts in trying to get the bridge project off the ground, many nights spent searching on the Internet. But then it suddenly occurred to me . . . I was trying to do it all on my own. The number of prayers I had offered on behalf of the bridge project I could count on one hand. For this project to be successful, that had to change. This *was* turning out to be a faith project, whether I wanted it to or not. I wasn't sure what God had in plan for this project or what the extent of my involvement would be, but I needed, once and for all, to turn it all over to Him.

As the invitation hymn began to play, I was reminded it was my Sunday to help set up the visitor table outside. The visitor table allows guests to receive a bag which contains information about our church, a prayer guide, and the church's newsletter. I quickly made my way outside to help another deacon set up the table and the bags. Then I realized that for me to go down to the altar, I would have to enter through the main sanctuary doors, and walk down the long aisle in front of everyone. Going forward during the altar call was not something I did regularly, probably not even once a year. But maybe this was His plan, for me to confess my lack of faith in front of witnesses. Walking up to the sanctuary doors, I peered through one window to see if the congregation was still singing . . . and they were. I eased the door open as quietly as I could, slipped inside, and slowly closed it behind me.

Pastor Ben at first didn't see me, as I slowly made my way down to the front of the sanctuary. I was definitely a bit nervous. As I took Pastor Ben's hand and leaned in towards him, I confessed my lack of faith. I also confessed the reason the bridge project was no farther along than a year ago was because I was trying to do it all, but now I was turning it all over to God because I had accomplished nothing on my own. I told him about the article on Bridges to Prosperity, and to pray for a response to a four page letter I had e-mailed to Avery and Ken the night before. I also asked him to pray for me.

CHAPTER TWO

An Answered Prayer

Going forward that Sunday was not only a turning point for the bridge, but for me spiritually as well. I felt that a huge burden had been lifted off my chest. I now understood what people mean when they say, "Turn it all over to God" and "Take your burdens to the altar and leave them there."

This reminded me of a hymn the choir would sing almost every Sunday at Jones Crossroads Baptist Church in Lancaster: "Tell It to Jesus." It's funny how we seem to remember the words to a familiar hymn, but not always the meaning of those words. The first part of verse one says, "Are you weary, are you heavy hearted? Tell it to Jesus, Tell it to Jesus." Now I finally understood the meaning of those words—"When our load is heavy and we are physically and mentally exhausted / Tell it to Jesus / He will listen / He will give you strength / He will ease your burden."

All day Monday at work, and even that night when taking my son, Jordan, to baseball practice, I reflected back on my prayer. Pulling into the baseball field parking lot, I felt my phone vibrate, which meant I had just gotten an e-mail. I waited until Jordan had gotten out of the truck, knowing an e-mail this late at night was probably a power outage alarm from work.

Taking my phone out of my pocket, I selected the "check e-mail" icon. It showed one unopened e-mail . . . an e-mail from KEN FRANTZ!! Opening the e-mail, I noticed it was not a form letter from a big company, but a personal letter written by Ken himself, as the first sentence stated, "I read your letter attached." Words cannot describe the emotions that ran through my body at that moment as tears covered my face and joy filled my heart. I immediately stopped and thanked God for the answer to my prayer, thanking Him for showing me an open door, one that I had searched for over a year on my own.

I called Pastor Ben to tell him this incredible news. He wasn't at home, so I managed to compose myself enough to leave him a message. Then I received a second e-mail from Bridges to Prosperity, this one from Milosz. I was simply amazed. That night I e-mailed a friend, telling about the answered prayer.

Crystal,

God has answered our prayers! If I wasn't directly involved with this project I would not have believed it! Incredible! I now have a national team wanting to look at our bridge site. I was literally in tears as I read the reply to my four page letter. I told Pastor Ben I want to share it this Sunday with our congregation . . . it's that big!

Thomas

P. S. I am going to suggest to our church's mission team our efforts be called "Bridge to Faith," because that's what projects like this do, they "bridge" our faith to God.

I spent the next night on Bridges to Prosperity's website, studying their bridge design manual, construction drawings and photos. Building a pedestrian walking bridge was still not going to be easy, but I felt encouraged as I looked at pictures of all the completed bridges on their website. Then, as I glanced back through the e-mail sent to me by Milosz, one of his statements struck me: "B2P does not fund bridges, nor do we do fundraising. The funds for the bridge must come from your church, the municipality, or a combination."

In their e-mails, Ken and Milosz had mentioned the estimated cost for the bridge of $25,000. This would be my church's portion of the project, to pay for the materials needed to build the bridge. Bridges to Prosperity would provide the final bridge design, training and supervision, which cost them about $25,000 per bridge. According to Ken, their bridge projects were sponsored by a Rotary club of their choosing, and that is where they get their money to provide the support for each project.

I spent the rest of the week preparing a message to share with my church congregation, giving a project update on the Bridge to Faith, with a theme of "Faith is you taking the first step, with Jesus ready to take your hand and lead you the rest of the way" accompanied by a verse of Scripture from the book of James: *"My brothers and sisters, if people say they have faith, but do nothing, their faith is worth nothing. Can faith like that save them?"* (James Chapter 2, Verse 14 NCV)

It had been over two years since Mike had introduced the project to the congregation, so part of my update re-introduced the purpose of the bridge and how it would help the community in Nicaragua. I included information about the organization Bridges to Prosperity, with whom I was recommending our mission team partner. I also gave them a construction time line, with an estimated completion date of May of 2011. Then, I asked for everyone's support for the project and prayer for other churches to join us in the fundraising, not just for the money, but to share in the blessings we would all receive when the project is completed, when we see a community of people standing on that bridge praising God.

I shared a lot of information with the church congregation that Sunday morning, except for one detail—the cost. A bridge fundraising campaign to raise $25,000; now how well would that go over with my congregation? Sure, the Nicaragua Mission Team had always been able to raise several thousand dollars each year for its small building projects, but never an amount even close to the $25,000 needed for the bridge. Plus, the church was in the middle of a challenge-to-build program for a new family life center. But before Mike or anyone else was going to announce the money part, we needed to meet a representative from Bridges to Prosperity in Nicaragua to determine if our bridge site would even meet the B2P criteria, not just in terms of soil conditions, but also the elevations.

CHAPTER THREE

FORGIVENESS

Turning it all over to God . . . to me this simply meant the bridge project. But not to God . . . He wanted more. After giving the first bridge update to my congregation that Sunday, I began to feel something stirring in my heart. I already felt my involvement in the bridge project bringing me closer to God.

On Tuesday, March 30th, I finished typing a sermon I had been working on all month. I titled it *The Faith Message*, based on the Gospel of Matthew Chapter 14, where Jesus calls Peter to step out of the boat and come to Him on the water. The sermon was filled with examples from my own life, situations where I had stepped out on faith to help someone in need, trusting for God to take control of the circumstances. The sermon's emphasis is that "faith is you taking the first step, with Jesus ready to take your hand and lead you the rest of the way." I intended to share the message with other church congregations, simply to encourage people to "step out on faith" and help others in this world, even in small ways. And yes, encourage them to support the bridge project in Nicaragua.

I read back over the sermon several times. Then it occurred to me: *The bridge in Nicaragua, what would be my part? What would be my step of faith?* As I continued to sit at the computer, my thoughts became focused on the friends who had passed away the year before, and just how short life really is. *When I die, what would people remember about me? Will I be remembered for what I had accomplished at my job? Is this it, is this all there is to life—money and daily routines?* As I searched for answers in my mind, I unknowingly fell into a deep sleep.

I had a vision: *At the age of 60, I died and went to Heaven. I found myself face-to-face with Jesus. Looking into my eyes, He asked me one question, "Twenty years ago I gave you this vision, and now, who have you helped in the past twenty years?" Thinking back, my eyes quickly fell away from His face; my head hung low as I answered, "No one, Lord . . . no one." He simply said, "Then go back and start telling the stories I will give to you, tell others about Me, and help as many people as you can."*

As I awoke, somewhat startled, I realized I was still only 40. Then I began to type, and this IS what I typed: *In my life, it's been tough getting to the top, having to paddle very hard. Now I'm at the top of my career and what I set out to achieve in my career. All that appears to be left is the slow ride down the middle of the river. 40 life years gone—20 good life years left. 17 career years gone—20 career years left, but what will be different then from now, what more is there to accomplish at my job? . . . nothing. Oh, [. . .] more money, but what do I need that I do not already have? . . . nothing, absolutely nothing. I am happy now, the happiest I have ever been in my entire life. But will I continue to be happy, knowing that I didn't help more people along the way, like I have such a passion to do?*

Then why not look for another mountain to climb. Oh, that would require leaving the safety of the boat, which is moving slowly down the middle of life's stream. That would mean getting out of the boat and into the water, going onto the shore . . . danger, unknowns, perils, falls, trips, etc.

Building the bridge in Nicaragua—I feel like I have one foot out of the boat, but what will it take to move the other, could it be the Bridge to Faith? Is that the mountain I want to climb, my final mountain? But what's on the other side, possibly more blessings from God, blessings beyond comprehension? What am I afraid of? Oh, I know, leaving the boat and getting out into the water, and having to fight the current to swim to shore. Then the people in the boat will be yelling, "Why did he leave the safety of the boat? What was he thinking?" To which my reply will be, "I had to, I needed another mountain to climb!" I wasn't going to simply waste the life I have left going through the daily routines, weekly routines, monthly routines, yearly routines. This is why I left the boat, to re-discover what life is about, helping other people.

After I had finished typing, I went into the living room and fell down on my knees at the sofa and poured my heart out to God. I prayed for God to show me what He wanted with my life. I asked Him to show me His purpose for my life, and to provide me a mountain to climb, a challenge in my life.

That night I had a dream. I was in a large body of water. Satan had thrown chains around my body and was dragging me down . . . I was drowning. I struggled to fight free, but couldn't. Satan was dragging me all the way to the bottom, and there was nothing I could do. I knew this was spiritual warfare, and it was *my life* that was caught in the battle.

As I looked toward the surface one last time, staring into a bright light, I saw a hand reaching down. I grabbed hold. As He began to pull me towards the surface, Satan's chains began to break. At last, I was free.

I remember waking up and being completely terrified at what I had just dreamed.

As I thought about the dream, I knew exactly what it meant. Even though I had been a confessing Christian since the age of 13, I had never fully committed my life to Christ and His purposes. This is what God wanted, for me to turn my whole life over to Him. I had tithed and attended church services, revivals and Bible studies most of my life. I had served as a deacon at Jones Crossroads Baptist Church in Lancaster and now at Sandy Level Baptist Church in Blythewood. But these things were not enough. With the upcoming trip to Nicaragua, I knew I needed to get my heart right with God. If I was going to be a witness to others, I first needed to get the plank out of my own eye.

The next evening, March 31st, after looking in a photo album for a special picture from a college mission trip, I saw a boy I did not know—someone maybe with the same name, but not the same person. I stared at myself in those pictures and thought, *Who was I?* Also in the bookcase were the middle school and high school annuals. I opened one and saw all those people who laughed at my Bobo shoes in elementary school (the colorful $10 ones from the discount store), the shoes worn because that was all my parents could afford.

Then I recalled the teasing I got in middle school for wearing old jeans that were too short, better known as high waters, because my parents only bought me new jeans at the beginning of each school year; and the boy who told me I was adopted because my mother didn't want me. The more I looked, the more things popped in my head, all the put-downs that caused me to harbor so many hurt feelings in my heart towards others. The resentment I felt towards all those people. My heart was full of it. I remembered each episode—even the names and faces of those kids who said them. In my heart I had never forgiven any of them.

Even at Regan's funeral, a school friend who passed away in 2009, I recognized everyone who was there that day, even kids not in my grade. But as I passed by each of them, not one person spoke to me first. I went up to several people and called them by name, but nobody recognized me until after I told them mine.

Later that evening as I left for choir practice, I buried these thoughts deep in my heart, promising myself I would never think about them again, but just move on. But at choir practice as we sang the last song, the words and message to that song went straight to my heart. I thought my heart was going to explode. It couldn't hold anymore—it was packed full of stuff I had held onto all my life. Something had to give.

After I got home, I went straight upstairs and threw them all out—all the school annuals with all those people in it and a photo album from my teenage years, because they brought it all back . . . all those painful memories. I guess everyone has his or her own way of dealing with things in life, but this was my way of dealing with mine. My wife said those were just kids back then, and that was my life, my memories—and I said, "No! I don't want to remember who I was—I'm not the same person."

Then I shared with her what I wrote. This was my way of putting it all in perspective: "In life, it's not important if someone doesn't recognize you for the boy you were; but when you speak your name, they embrace the man you've become. A man who is a faithful husband to his wife, a nurturing father to his children, but most importantly . . . a follower of God's will."

I dug everything out of my heart that night, giving it all up. For once in my life, I had come to grips with my past. In my heart, I forgave all of those kids. Forgiveness, we all need to give it, and I am so glad I finally did. I now felt a lot different inside, like my heart had just been washed clean. It was a feeling I had never felt before, maybe because I couldn't remember ever feeling any different.

Sunday, April 4th, was Easter Sunday. The sermon was on walls. Our youth pastor, Jake, did part one of the message, and he was speaking directly to me. It was just what I needed to hear. Walls in our lives (MY LIFE), walls we (I) cannot move past, not without His (JESUS') help. Then I began to realize that all my life, I had built so many walls in my heart. All the stuff I had dug out of my heart, everything I had given up can be summarized in one word—"WALL."

The second part of the message focused on personal walls, and to break through my personal walls, I need the resurrection power of Jesus. The resurrection power is available through faith. My internal walls (the ones built in my heart) will:

1. No longer control me (and my emotions)
2. No longer dominate me (and my life)

During the altar call, I went forward and taped a piece of paper on the wall setup beside the pulpit. I wrote the words "My Past" on it. At that moment, I felt the walls in my heart come crumbling down. I had finally overcome the things in my life that were holding me back from truly living and had found real peace. It made me realize that continuing to think about the events in my past was meaningless.

CHAPTER FOUR

TEN ONE-DOLLAR BILLS

With everything that happened in my spiritual life during the month of March, I finally felt prepared for the trip to Nicaragua. I had turned the bridge project completely over to God, received an answer from Bridges to Prosperity, and had finished *The Faith Message.*

But less than two weeks before my first trip to Nicaragua, an unfortunate accident had left a friend lying in a hospital bed with a fractured neck. Richard was lucky to be alive after crashing his motorcycle in a shallow ditch off Highway 555 near Blythewood, narrowly avoiding a head-on collision with an oncoming car.

My friendship with Richard originated at the baseball fields in Blythewood when our sons started playing tee ball. They had even played on the same team two seasons. Most of our conversations centered on baseball, though a few years back we discussed his job and a building expansion at the large distribution center where he worked, and how the power was going to be routed to serve the new expansion. But now it was much more serious than baseball or electricity—the doctors did not know how much damage had been done to the vertebrae in his neck or the recovery prognosis.

After finishing supper on a Wednesday night, I decided to go and visit Richard and his family at the hospital. I planned to stop by the store to pick up a few items for my wife, Cynthia, and purchase a *Get Well* card for Richard. But just before leaving, I heard His voice say, "Take them ten one-dollar bills." I was startled. I almost asked the Lord why now, because I had never shared that story with anyone, not even my dad. And why, after twenty years, would the Lord be telling me to share that blessing now, with this family, and not with a relative who might better understand its meaning? So, not wanting to feel foolish, I told Cynthia what I planned to do. She gave me a bewildered look of, "That sounds kind of weird."

But without her having to say a word, I started explaining its personal significance.

In 1989, during the week of Thanksgiving, my mother was in the hospital quickly losing her battle with breast cancer. After being in remission for almost two years, the cancer had come back, but this time it was deemed terminal. As a 20-year-old, this news was hard to take, especially with the upcoming Thanksgiving and Christmas holidays.

That Monday night, my Uncle Robert, my dad's brother, and I walked out of the hospital together, and as we stopped at his car in the parking lot, he turned to me with a very serious look, and told me words that I will never forget. He said, "Tommy, your mother loves you very much, and the only reason she is still alive today is because of wanting to see you. But we both know she's not going to get any better, so you have to pray to God for Him to take her home now." There, standing in the middle of that hospital parking lot, I prayed the hardest prayer I have ever prayed in my entire life.

The next day, the extended family was called in for one last visit. As I sat alone in the waiting room studying, trying not to flunk out of my junior year at Clemson, the family members from Richburg and Edgemoor arrived. As each cousin passed by me to speak, my Aunt Ethel stopped and handed me an envelope. Though it was the first card I had received while at the hospital, I was not surprised since she was always doing special things for people. I was a little curious as she stood in front of me while I opened the envelope, almost waiting to see my reaction as I read the card for the first time.

As I pulled the card from the envelope and opened it to read, there appeared before my eyes some dollar bills. As I counted them, there were exactly ten . . . ten one-dollar bills. I softly exclaimed, "Thank you," though my face may have still had the look of surprise on it. Smiling from ear to ear, she simply replied, "You're going to be here all week, and sometimes you may not be able to find change for the drink or cracker machine."

That was it. Though not the biggest or most expensive gift I had ever received, exactly what I needed at that moment, which admittedly was one of the lowest in my young adult life. Just a simple gift that said, "Hey, I care about you."

It had been over twenty years, but I remembered receiving that card with those ten one-dollar bills from my aunt like it was yesterday. And even though those ten one-dollar bills meant so much to me back then, I had never felt the need to ever share that blessing with anyone else, until now. Not stopping to ask any more questions, I was convinced that now was the time to finally share that blessing with another person and their family, who may need just a simple expression of "Hey, I care."

As I finished telling Cynthia the story, she was speechless. I told her I knew I had never shared that story with her, and frankly didn't remember sharing it with anyone else either. It was just a special moment that was significant to me, but no one else would ever find it meaningful unless they had been there that day.

So there it was . . . the story of the ten one-dollar bills, brought back to life for the first time in over twenty years. Though at the time I had no idea why, a smile consumed me just thinking about the surprise on Richard's face when he would open the card. Making people smile . . . that's what I enjoy most in life.

Just as I had already planned, I stopped by the store in Blythewood to pick up a few items and a *Get Well* card for Richard. Taking time to pick out the right card was somewhat important, but remembering to get cash back at the checkout counter, including asking the cashier for ten one-dollar bills, was top priority. So, as I stepped in line behind a few others, I went ahead and took out my wallet to make sure I pulled out my debit card, and not the credit card, like I'm in the habit of doing. I admit I was a bit nervous, even wondering if the cashier would even question why I was asking for ten one-dollar bills and a ten. I worried about what she would think of me for making such a strange request. So, here I go once again, worrying about what people would be thinking about me for doing something "out of the ordinary."

"Next please," was the phrase the cashier used to get my attention. As I pushed my items forward, I placed the *Get Well* card on top of the box of cake rolls, a staple food item for me and my son, Jordan. As she finished scanning the last few items, she politely asked me, "Anything else?" As I swiped my debit card, I was careful to remember to select the "cash back" option when prompted on the touch screen. Asking for cash back was something I did only once in a blue moon, if even that often. Cash back <select> . . . twenty dollars <select> . . . done.

As she went to access her cash drawer, I promptly spoke up and said, "I would like a ten and ten one-dollar bills, please." I admit, she did give me a slight look of "strange," but pulled out her ones and counted out ten, then grabbed a ten and the register receipt and handed them to me and politely told me, "Thank you."

Driving down the Interstate, my thoughts raced forward to the hospital visit with Richard and his family. What would I say, what questions would

I ask, but more importantly, at what point during my visit would I give him the card with those ten one-dollar bills inside? And, if he opened it immediately in front of everyone, how they would react when they saw the ten one-dollar bills . . . and what they would think about the meaning?

As I pulled into the hospital parking lot, I quickly put all of those thoughts in the back of my mind and pulled myself together, since just thinking about what I was about to do brought back so many painful memories for me. But just remembering what a small blessing those ten one-dollar bills were to me back then, and now, over twenty years later, feeling led to finally share that blessing with a friend . . . that brought a smile to my face.

Finally finding a parking spot, I pulled out my wallet and counted out ten one-dollar bills, carefully arranging them in the card. I wrote a little note explaining their meaning, and placed the card in the envelope. But before I could seal it, I heard His voice again say, "Give them the rest." So without even hesitating, I pulled the card back out and inserted the ten dollar bill with the other bills and sealed the envelope.

Entering the hospital, I was so nervous about the card I almost didn't remember his last name when prompted by the receptionist at the desk. Luckily, Richard's last name is a lot like his first, so I recalled it quickly. I clutched the envelope as I made my way up to his room, all the way trying not to forget the room number.

Upon entering his room, I was surprised to see him sitting up in bed and with no broken limbs, though he wore a neck brace to keep his head from turning. His wife, Jeannie, and son, Jacob, were in the room, along with another lady who I believe was Jeannie's sister. He looked surprised to see me, but at the same time glad to see a friend from the baseball field. I talked with them for about twenty minutes, mostly with Jeannie, about his neck injury, possible surgery, and recovery. The outcome looked very promising, considering how close Jeannie said he came to being paralyzed. The paramedics told them that one wrong turn of his neck at the accident scene, and the broken vertebrae would have severed his spinal cord, causing irreversible damage. Jeannie told me that even though he didn't have any external injuries from the accident, the paramedics at the accident scene that evening took all the right precautions with him. She thanked God for the right people being there that evening.

Checking my watch for the fourth time, I told them I had to be at choir practice at 7:45 p.m., since we were singing at the Cedar Creek Baptist Church on Monday night. So, as I said my final good-bye, I slowly pulled out the envelope. I could see Jeannie's eyes immediately focus on it, so I quickly handed it to her. I told them it wasn't much, and they never even needed to thank me for it. They thanked me for coming, and I quietly shut the door as I left, but not before taking a quick peek to see if she had begun to open the envelope—she hadn't.

Making my way out to my truck, I was very nervous about what I had just done, even having the thought, *They've opened the card, and now they're looking out the window at me wondering what type of guy would do something like this.* Anyways, it was done. I had followed through on what I was told to do, and had passed the blessing of the ten one-dollar bills on to someone else. Seeing the look of surprise on their faces as I handed Jeannie the envelope with the card inside, well, that's a moment I knew I would not soon forget. Plus, I felt good inside for what I had done.

Author's Comments: Now, I know you may be wondering why this isn't the end of the book? This, my friend, is only the beginning of the journey.

CHAPTER FIVE

"Man, You're an Angel"

As I left the hospital parking lot that Wednesday night, I knew it was the Lord who had told me to share those ten one-dollar bills with Richard and his family. For what reason, at that moment, I did not know. And as I drove on Highway 277 back to Blythewood, in the distance I saw a woman standing beside her car in the grassed median. As I passed, I quickly glanced and saw what appeared to be a flat tire. But stopping to help would mean being late for choir practice. So with that in mind, I reluctantly passed by the next opportunity to turn around, and simply reassured myself that someone else would stop and help her. Though this was not the first time I had not stopped and helped someone, it reminded me of the blessing I received from a person whom I *had* stopped and helped.

It was the weekend of Cynthia's parents' 50th Wedding Anniversary, and I was heading back to Blythewood from Lexington early that warm Sunday morning. As I was about to exit off of I-20 onto Highway 277, I said a simple prayer, "Lord, please show me someone to help today." As I went around the off-ramp, I looked to my left and saw a man walking with a small plastic gas can. He was wearing an old T-shirt with a large gamecock emblem on the front and cutoff blue jeans.

I stopped on the shoulder of the exit ramp and rolled down my window, but waited for him to get closer before speaking. Seeing I had stopped and appeared willing to help, he smiled and simply shouted, "Hey!" Being a Clemson Alumnus and somewhat of a jokester, I shouted back to him, "I was going to help you, but when I saw what kind of shirt you were wearing, now I'm not!" Not breaking stride, he glanced down at what was on the front of his shirt, and then gave me a look back like "what?!" By this time he had gotten closer to where I was parked, so I showed him a smile and said, "Come on . . . get in."

He said he'd walked about two miles from his truck, and no one else had stopped to offer help. He said he really appreciated me stopping. He told me the gas gauge in his truck was broken and he thought he had enough to make it to the bank, where he was going to get some money to buy more gas for his truck. As we talked, I could tell he was telling the truth, because he was hot and sweaty from the long walk. I asked him if he had any money for the gas, to which he replied he didn't, but if I would loan him a few dollars he would pay me back once he went to the bank.

As we rode to the gas station, I asked him, "Hey, are you a Christian?" (You can talk to someone about anything when he is riding in the backseat of your air conditioned truck and needs gas.) His answer was a shocking one, "I used to be." I immediately turned and asked him what he meant by that statement. He said he was saved once, but all his friends ever told him was since he sinned everyday, he needed to be re-saved everyday, and if he didn't, he was not a Christian anymore, and would not go to heaven if he died at that moment.

Looking in the rearview mirror, I told him if he believed Jesus was the Son of God, died on the cross for his sins, and on the third day arose from the dead, and he invited Jesus into his heart, then he WAS a Christian, and his name IS written in the Lambs Book of Life, FOREVER! He stared at me in the mirror and softly said, "No one has ever told me that . . . I am so glad you stopped to help me." I could see the tears as they began to stream down his cheeks, right there in the backseat of my truck, as I slowly moved the mirror so he couldn't see mine. Gaining back my composure, I told him we all sin everyday, and need the forgiveness of Jesus everyday, and when we ask for it, He will give it.

After a few minutes, I turned and asked him where his bank was located, and did he just want me to take him there to get some money for his gas? Laughing slightly, he replied, "You didn't understand me. I am divorced and have been laid off from my land surveying job for over a year now. I was going to the blood bank where I've been told I can get $50 for my platelets." Oh, now I understood completely his situation, and quickly thought to myself, *His gas gauge isn't broke . . . but he is.* And seeing how moments before I had helped heal his spiritual brokenness, I knew I could do something to help his financial brokenness too.

Soon, we exited off the highway and onto Parklane Road, where I pulled into the gas station. I got his five-gallon gas can from the back of my truck and took it over to the pump, swiped my credit card, and began to fill it with fuel. After only a few dollars, he began to say, "That's enough, that's enough." I turned to him and replied, "It will be enough when it's full." The pump shut off and I rounded the amount to an even $12. As we got back in to leave, I could see he looked worried—maybe about how he was going to pay me back. I was prepared for that.

As we passed by his truck, parked on the other side of the four-lane highway, he said, "Just let me out here, you've done enough, I can walk back to my truck." I told him, "No, I've got to turn around anyways . . . it's not out of my way at all. Besides, I've taken you this far." He didn't have anything to say after that, but just sat there with a blank stare until we had turned around and made it back to his truck.

Getting the gas can from the back of my truck for him, I asked if he needed any more help. He said that I had done enough. We exchanged names and a handshake, and as I went to walk off, he said, "Hey, I need your address so I can send you the money to repay you for the gas." I'm not sure where these words came from as I replied, "If I give you my address then you will be worrying about when you're going to get the money to repay me, and I'll be worrying about when you are." Then he looked me straight in the eyes and said something that no one had ever said to me, "Man, you're an angel." Pulling away, I simply smiled and waved as I left him filling his truck's gas tank.

Driving on to church in Blythewood, those words resonated in my mind and left me wondering why he would say such words to me. Maybe because it was Sunday morning and nobody else had stopped to help him . . . a man wearing an old T-shirt and cutoff blue jeans walking on the side of the highway with a gas can. But then I reminded myself I was only being obedient to the simple question I had asked earlier, "Lord, show me someone to help today."

Sometimes I wonder whatever happened to that man, if he found a job, or if he's now sharing Christ's love and forgiveness with his friends. Maybe even telling them of the stranger who picked him up from the side of the highway one Sunday morning and who shared the good news of Christ with him. I will always remember this story as long as I live, inspiring me to always do more for others than I do for myself.

And just like with the $20 I had given to Richard and his family, I would never miss the $12 spent buying a complete stranger fuel that Sunday morning either. And re-living that story in my mind made me almost miss the Blythewood Road exit from the Interstate. But regardless, I was still my usual five minutes late to Wednesday night choir practice, a habit that I just couldn't seem to break.

CHAPTER SIX

The Abney Level

Choir practice went well that Wednesday night, and I looked forward to singing one of my favorite songs, "Midnight Cry," at the revival service at Cedar Creek Baptist Church on Monday night. But even after a busy evening, I still had one more item to purchase before leaving on my trip to Nicaragua, which was just over a week away. Getting out the phonebook, I looked up the number for a friend's business, a business that he actually operates out of his house. I had come across his business in the phonebook weeks before while spending time with my dad.

When I had called the business that Friday I noticed it was located in Cedar Creek, a community only a few miles from my subdivision. So when the person answered, "This is Eddie," I immediately recognized his voice. We had not talked in years, so we spent several minutes catching up a little—his job, my job, etc.

Then I explained the reason for calling. I was going to survey a bridge site in Nicaragua, and I needed a small survey instrument the Bridges to Prosperity bridge design manual refers to as an Abney Level. Now, being an electrical engineer, I had no idea what this instrument looked like, so I had researched it on the Internet so I could at least talk somewhat intelligently, in case no one else had ever heard of it, either.

But this time when I called Eddie, I had the manufacturer and model number of the Abney Level I wanted to purchase, and had noted the list price on the Internet was around $100. Thankfully, the manufacturer was a brand Eddie sold, so all he needed was the model number. Finishing up our conversation, I mentioned that the Sandy Level Baptist Church's choir would be singing at his church's revival service on Monday night, and he could give me the Abney Level then, and I would bring him a check—he agreed.

With the anticipation for my trip the following week, the weekend seemed to be a blur, and before I knew it, it was Monday night. I actually arrived early to the revival service, hoping to talk with Eddie and see if he had the Abney Level. He hadn't called me that day as promised to let me know if the Abney Level was in or not, so I was a bit worried. I was a little disappointed when I didn't see him. But as the choir was being seated in the choir loft, I quickly spotted him seated in the congregation.

After performing our song, the choir exited and found what seating was available among the congregation. Of course, since we were in a Baptist church, there were plenty of available seats on the first two pews. I was surprised when I noticed several empty seats on the pew where Eddie and his wife were seated. I felt uneasy enough singing in a church other than my own, so being able to sit with a friend during the message time made me feel a little more at ease.

My pastor preached a great sermon, and I distinctly remember being more focused on the message than usual, paying attention to every word and letting his words penetrate my heart with the power of God's Word. Maybe it was the weeks of preparing my heart for Nicaragua, for the mission work that lay ahead, or of the newfound sense of purpose in my life. In what seemed to be only five minutes, the traditional altar call was being sung. But instead of going forward for prayer, I simply stood quietly in the pew, staring at the back of the church.

Then I closed my eyes and silently prayed for God to take my hand and lead me in what I considered to be a huge step of faith. "Stepping out of the boat," a phrase I had coined in *The Faith Message* written in March, came to mind. I recalled the story of Jesus calling Peter to step out of the boat and come to him on the water. But even with that thought, I was still carrying one unanswered prayer in my heart, *Am I called by God to build bridges in third world countries?*

After the service, I was finally able to speak with Eddie concerning the Abney Level. I got a little worried when he told me that it didn't ship from the factory until this morning, but did feel a little better when he said it was scheduled to be here on Wednesday. Even if it was late, this meant I should still get it by Friday, my departure date. I guess he read the concern on my face as he told me he would drop it by my office as soon as it arrived at his house. This did ease my tension, as I already had enough things to worry about remembering for the trip, and this would be one less.

As we continued to talk, I slowly pulled out my wallet. As I reached in to pull out one of the new one hundred-dollar bills I had got from the bank on Friday, he shocked me with the statement, "No, you don't owe me anything . . . it's my donation to the trip." That stopped me in my tracks, because I'm the one who is always sharing my loaf with others, and not the other way around. But being on the receiving end of someone else's generosity made me realize how the people I help must feel inside, and my handshake of appreciation for his generosity and a sincere "Thank you" were all he needed in return.

By the time we had finished talking business that night, almost everyone had left to go home. Then I remembered I had not been able to give my offering when the plate was passed during the service, so was sure to catch the gentleman as he was going to count it. Plus, I had just received an unexpected blessing of generosity from a friend, so I made a special effort to return a portion to God's house.

Finally making my way to the exit, I stopped to shake hands with the church's pastor. I briefly shared with him about my trip to Nicaragua at the end of the week, and the need for the pedestrian bridge. He seemed quite interested, and told me he would pray for Mike and me to have a safe trip. I thanked him, and made my way to the parking lot.

At my truck, I got a lonely feeling inside, almost like I wanted someone to stop and pray for me before I left for my trip. But by this time everyone had left, except for one person, Bob. Bob and I share a special bond—we are late to everything. So as Bob came over to speak, I made a joke by saying, "Well, I guess we are late coming and late going." He looked at me and smiled . . . then we both laughed.

Then Bob asked, "Hey Thomas, you're leaving for Nicaragua this Friday, right?" Nonchalantly I said, "Yes, that's right." His next words were a complete surprise, "Then I would like to pray for you right now." As he prayed from his heart, I almost couldn't hold back the tears. He prayed, "Lord, I ask that you be with Thomas and Mike as they travel to Nicaragua. I pray for their safety as they travel, and I pray that they be able to accomplish all the work they need to for the bridge. Lord, I thank you for giving Thomas the knowledge and ability he needs for this project—and the desire to go and follow your will. AMEN." Then he said a few final words of encouragement followed by the statement, "Thomas, people need to see God move."

As I drove from the church parking lot that night, I began to search through my mind for what Bob meant by that statement. Did he mean people needed to see something happen that only God could allow to happen, or did he mean people needed to see God move in my life, and if that be the case, then how?

With those thoughts now fresh in my mind, I started to sense something really great happening on my trip, maybe at the bridge site. Although I was worried about all the logistics of the trip, I began to sense that God was in the midst of it all, and that all I needed to do was be willing to "step out of the boat" and go. I knew that just committing to go to Nicaragua meant I had one foot out of the boat, but what would it take to move the other?

And again, the question that kept resonating in my mind was, *Is God calling me to third world countries, and if He is, is it to build these bridges?* I was definitely interested in the bridge project since it would be helping a whole community of people, but the only way to know if I was "called" was to get on that airplane Friday morning to go and find out.

CHAPTER SEVEN

AM I CALLED?—THE ANSWER

Before I knew it, it was Friday morning, and Mike and I were on I-77 headed to the Charlotte-Douglas Airport. With our busy work schedules, we hadn't had many opportunities to talk about the trip. We made small talk most of the way, except at one point Mike became a little more serious. "Thomas," he said, "look in the mirror . . . you will not be the same person when you get back." As I heard those words, I thought I knew what he meant. I had never been to a developing country. I would be exposed to poverty and living conditions like I had never seen. Honestly, I wasn't really sure what to expect.

It wasn't until on the flight from Miami to Nicaragua that I became more focused on the purpose of the trip. My mind raced forward to meeting Avery, meeting with the community at the bridge site, and finally, whether or not God would provide me with an answer to my question, *Am I called?* I had specifically asked God for a physical sign and not just a feeling in my heart. I wanted a sign so that if someone ever asked me if I was called to build these bridges, I could provide them with a definite answer: "Yes!"

About an hour into the flight, I decided to pull out a small, pocket size devotional book to read. It was a forty day devotional book I had picked up at church two weeks before the trip, but had not yet opened. I briefly stopped to ask God to bless the trip, to pray for our safety, and to thank Him for this opportunity to reach out to help others. I slowly opened the small devotional book to DAY 1. When I saw the Scripture passage, tears streamed down my face. I slowly shook my head in disbelief as I wiped away the tears. The devotion was based on the Gospel of Matthew Chapter 14, where Jesus calls Peter out of the boat.

I now had the answer to my prayer, and it came as a physical sign just like I had asked. Though not as dramatic as the burning bush as seen by

Moses in the Bible, it was the clearest sign I had ever received from God in my life.

I spent the remainder of the flight reading the other days' devotions. At some point, I noticed the lady beside me had become interested in what I was reading. Wanting to be a witness for Christ, I let her read along as I read each devotional aloud. She was from Nicaragua and spoke some English, but I wasn't sure how well she could read it. I didn't think much about this until I later learned she was a Jehovah's Witness.

As the pilot lowered the plane's altitude in preparation for landing, I peered out the window to see the country of Nicaragua for my first time. As I gazed at the mountains covered with thick green forests, the lady turned to me and said, "My country is very beautiful . . . but very poor." Wow, what a profound statement.

After slowly making our way through Customs and airport security, I quickly turned my attention to finding Avery. Her flight should have arrived two hours before ours, so it was no telling where she might be. I told her in an e-mail that I would be wearing a Clemson hat, which I thought would be easy to spot in Nicaragua. There were a lot of people waiting for their families and others holding up signs with names on them, but Avery was nowhere to be seen. The success of this trip depended on her being able to receive the airline ticket in Guatemala I had bought on-line the week before, then making the flight to Nicaragua.

As we continued through the airport, Mike saw Danilo. Danilo is Mike's long time Nicaraguan friend and the one who told Mike about the need for the pedestrian walking bridge. He was glad to see Mike, and happy to meet me, a person whom he felt brought hope to making his vision of a bridge a reality.

As we continued talking, Mike noticed a young woman sitting on a bench across the room. It was Avery! I'm not sure who was excited to see whom the most, but I was relieved that she had made the flight. After brief introductions, we gathered our luggage and started out towards Danilo's passenger van. As we walked, I began to have a strong feeling of this bridge project becoming an incredible story.

CHAPTER EIGHT

STORIES OF FAITH

Leaving the airport parking lot, I immediately began to take in all the scenery. There were people standing in the middle of the street selling small bags of water, juice, peanuts and fruit. And flea market type stands set up all along the roadside, with people selling everything from jewelry and clothes to name brand shoes. Then I saw what appeared to be hundreds of homemade tents covered with black plastic in a large open field, right in the middle of town. "Mike, what are those people doing there?" I asked.

After consulting with Danilo for several minutes, Mike turned to me and started telling those people's story. "A large banana grower has large plantations and it's customary to use the *campesinos*, the country people who are poorly educated and cheap labor. They sent them into the banana plantations with a pesticide called Nemagon, spraying the bananas without any personal protective equipment, and no information that it could be hazardous."

"Shortly thereafter these workers came down with all kinds of illnesses. The birth defects were horrible. In Costa Rica they have a museum of fetuses in jars of the birth defects. There were lawsuits brought about in all the countries, and they were settled everywhere except Nicaragua. The tent city was a protest . . . there was still more court action . . . they wanted help." After Mike had finished, I was speechless.

It wasn't long before we left the city and were on a more rural road. Oscar seemed to slow down and swerve to avoid every pothole that was in the road, even with oncoming traffic. It didn't take me long to get used to his driving.

As I continued to peer out my window from the backseat, I noticed along the roadside that people had built homes made of wooden sticks covered with plastic sheeting. I asked Mike who let these people build their homes so close to the road. Mike told me these people are very poor, do not own any land, and basically don't own anything but what's inside of that shelter. These squatters work to gather the sticks to make the frame, and then save the money they earn by working in the fields or even gathering firewood for other families. When they have enough money, they buy the plastic sheeting. Sometimes the plastic sheeting is donated by the government. If they are lucky and a piece of cardboard blows off a passing truck, then they can cover the dirt floor. Either way, it's wet when it rains, though with the cardboard floor, it's not as cold.

Mike then mentioned that when the city feels like there are too many of these people along the roadside, it will send a bulldozer and clean up the roadside in one day, piling up all the debris. These people generally have only minutes to gather everything they own, or at least what they have stored inside of their shelter. Then, once the bulldozer is gone, they start the endless process all over again.

I could hardly bear to hear any more as Mike continued by telling the next story. "A boy and a girl, they were coming up to the Bible study, lived in this little old . . . cardboard mess . . . down there up against the airport fence. Danilo's mom wanted us to donate just a few sheets of tin from our work project to help out this family. We went down there and it (the shelter) was a mess. One little old nasty piece of foam that the parents slept in, and over top of it there was like a hammock that the two kids slept in—a little boy about ten and a little girl about twelve. I couldn't stand up straight in there. So we went down there and said, 'Yeah, look, we can do something about this.' We tore it down and shot a black coral out of there—a very poisonous snake. It (the shelter) was just cardboard and junk . . . it was essentially trash. It was constructed of trash."

As we passed yet another group of these shelters, my heart almost broke, now knowing these people's struggles just to make it through one day. But even more than that, how we as Americans take so much for granted; even people who think they have nothing in America are rich compared to these people. All most people seem to think about is themselves and having fun, all while a world of people are struggling everyday just to survive, much less enjoy life.

As we continued on the three-hour trip northward into the mountains, Mike told of the city dump where our church's mission team had built a feeding shelter for the people living there. Bewildered, I asked Mike if he meant for the workers.

The next part of his story was hard for me to understand. "The feeding shelter was for the community of recyclers, people who go through the dump searching for tin, metal, or anything that they can sell. There's one place, I've been by there . . . just walking, they salvage plastic and wash plastic by hand in a washtub, and hang it up on a clothes line—and people buy it."

These people own practically nothing in this world. Mike explained that "the feeding shelter was built so the elderly and the children can get at least one meal a day, which is normally rice and a piece of bread. A lot of times it would be a tomato and an egg; it's better than starvation."

"There was a family whose kids would come to the feeding program and Bible study. And, of course, the dump is their playground, too. Someone had thrown rat poison out, or there had been rat poison in the trash. It was pink and the kids just associated the pink with candy, and ate it. One of the kids started getting violently ill, and the mother took the child and went to the hospital. Well about the time that child was dying, the father comes in with another one of their children, and about the time that child died, a neighbor came in with their last child . . . and that child died. They lost all their children."

"And some years ago, there was a dental x-ray machine thrown away. The part that contained the radioactive material was like a ball, and whoever the recycler was managed to break this ball. The dust, the radioactive material inside, it glows. They were superstitious and they rubbed it all over themselves, and they glowed and all that. It killed several children and gave some other people radiation poisoning."

After Mike told these stories, I remembered a lady at church telling me a story of the dump. Her husband had in fact been on the mission team that had built the feeding shelter. Though she didn't explain it in as much detail as Mike, she told it from her husband's viewpoint. I retold the story I had been told. "When you first see the dump, all you see is a large mound of trash. Then, as you get closer, you notice that it's moving. Getting even closer, you realize it's hundreds of people moving on the trash, scouring for food scraps, clothes, and any anything they can use to make improvements to their living shelter."

After I finished, everyone remained quiet, like each was still picturing this in their mind. Or maybe they were like me, overwhelmed with the sight of the poverty along the roadside as we passed. Then I began to wonder, *If life around the city of Managua was this bad, what would it be like up near the mountain town of Matiguas? Would it be this bad, and if so, would a pedestrian bridge make even a dent of an impact on their lives?*

We were less than an hour away from the town of Matiguas, and while Mike and Avery exchanged their views on world politics, I continued to process everything I had already seen and heard. It was almost overwhelming. I thought I was prepared, but I'm not sure anything could have prepared me for this experience.

Breaking a brief period of silence, Mike shared with us several stories of faith. Mike did not know that in my vision from God in March, Jesus had instructed me to ". . . go back and start telling the stories I will give to you . . ." At that time, I had no idea what His statement meant, but now it was becoming much clearer.

Many of Mike's stories came from a time when the country of Nicaragua was at war with itself. He told a story that came from his Nicaraguan friend, Pastor Henry. "Henry is Costa Rican, and being Costa Rican, he travelled pretty freely preaching during the war time, because he was a foreigner and not involved in the civil war. Henry told about a family—the father and son were combatants. The other side, their enemy, went to the home to kill them (the father and the son). The family was alerted to the approaching enemy, and the father and the son ran, leaving the mother and small children at home in the little shack. The shack was surrounded by the combatants, and they just chopped it to pieces with automatic weapon fire. When they stopped shooting, they went in and found the woman and her children around a little table . . . with a Bible . . . praying. They (the bullets) hadn't cut a hair—they were unharmed."

Then Mike began to tell the next story. "There was a lady, her name was Ruby. Ruby was a little black lady, about as wide as she was tall. She was from the blue fields, which is the Caribbean side (of Nicaragua). The black folks over there speak English; they are descendants of English slaves. Ruby had just tremendous faith. Ruby died last spring . . . she's been dead almost a year now. Ruby would pray for you . . . with just an uncanny personal knowledge of your needs. Some people criticized Ruby. People would go by there and she would pray for them and they would leave money. She lived on faith. She had no means of income. She prayed for people. The Lord sent people, she prayed for them, and they left her offerings and supported her. I don't care how you believe . . . I knew her . . . and she was just a tremendous woman."

"As I said, Ruby was from the blue fields, the Caribbean side, and the road to go over there is absolutely horrible. I have been as far as Bonanza on the road and that's halfway across, and is over twelve hours. There are holes in the road big enough to swallow a truck. If you get up to 35 mph on that cross country road, you are flying."

"The means of transportation for years has been riverboat. Ruby wanted to go home to visit from Managua. They would go down to Lake Nicaragua, tenth largest freshwater lake in the world, and get on a riverboat. The riverboat would go down the San Juan River and then back up the coast. This was the route that the 49ers took to California. Mark Twain took that route; would come up the San Juan River, and then it was—I think—a seventeen-mile stagecoach ride to the Pacific and get on a ship and go on up to California. At one point in time that was the shortest route . . . the quickest route."

"Ruby was on a large riverboat. They were on their way down the river, several people sitting on benches, so-on and so-forth. Ruby said that she was sitting beside a little girl, ten or eleven years old. She said they went around the bend in the river and a woman came out of a little small shack on the river bank with what appeared to be a dishpan and waved it in the air. Ruby said another woman beside her waved back. Ruby said she didn't know why, but she said, 'You shouldn't oughta done that.'"

"Well, they went around another bend (in the river), and there was machine gun fire from both side of the river. It (the waving dishpan) had been a signal. Ruby said that she just grabbed the little girl and rolled down on top of her. She didn't realize it at the time, but the boat's pilot had been killed and the Sandinista soldiers that were on the boat held her nephew at gun point and made him standup and navigate the boat while it was taking all the machine gun fire; it was either do that or they were going to kill him."

"Ruby said they got on through the (machine gun) fire; it was total chaos on the boat. She said during the (machine gun) fire the Lord had told her, 'Raise your hand to Me.' She said she raised her hand in the air. She said she felt something hit her hand—she just grasped it."

"Anyway, after they went around (the river) and got on away from the gun fire, she said there had been a group of Mexican laborers in the front of the boat—they were all killed. She said that people were just running all over the boat, and said someone came to her and said, '*Señora*, you are horribly wounded.' She said, 'No, I beg your pardon, I serve a great and powerful God.' The chaos and the screaming and wailing continued, and someone else came by and said, '*Señora*, you are horribly wounded.' She said, 'No, I beg your pardon, I serve a great and powerful God.' They came to the port and she said the Lord told her, 'You can lower your hand now.' She said she opened her eyes and the lady beside her who had waved at the woman on the (river) bank was dead. She said she looked in her hand, and she had a bullet in her hand."

After Mike had finished telling us those two stories, I continued to stare at him for a brief moment. I could tell he truly believed every word he was saying, every single detail. There was no doubt in my mind that God had protected these individuals from harm.

The trip to the Matiguas had been over three hours, and unfortunately, there were no fast food restaurants anywhere. The gas station we had stopped at was closed, but thankfully, attendants were still selling drinks from the outside coolers. Then I felt bad, remembering the only food items I had packed for the trip were crackers and Fig Newtons. Even though I had wanted to buy Avery a nice meal to show my appreciation for her being here, this was all I had to offer. For some reason, it didn't seem to matter to her.

A good meal was not the only thing. Since our bridge was not yet an official Bridges to Prosperity project, Avery could not turn in any of the expenses from this trip. This meant I had to agree upfront to cover all of her associated expenses, meaning meals, lodging, and a round trip airline ticket from Guatemala to Nicaragua. Knowing this was the open door for this project I had prayed, I walked through it, not fully knowing where I was going to get the extra money to pay for the $500 airline ticket.

Then I remembered the mission team meeting last year, when I had asked how we were going to raise the money for the bridge. Mike looked at me and said, "Have faith, God will provide the money." My immediate reply was, "But someone has to give the money, right?" He simply agreed and smiled, seeing my faith was still based on "seeing" and not "believing." So, not knowing anything else to do, I had prayed.

I prayed that week for my dad to give me a donation for the trip, even for a specific amount. Then, on Friday, my dad called me and we met for lunch in Blythewood. I told him the dates for my trip and everything I hoped to accomplish at the bridge site. He was very excited, and even mentioned he wished he had done more when he was my age, but now felt he was too old. We continued talking in the restaurant's parking lot. Then, as he went to get in his truck to leave, he suddenly stepped back out. He had his checkbook. He wrote me a check for $500. Avery's plane ticket was $503.

After hearing Mike's stories and seeing God move in the lives of these Nicaraguan people, and then remembering my own story, I began to wonder if most people in today's society are just too busy with their daily routines to see God move. If God moved in their life, would they even notice? Would I have? And receiving the answer to my question, *Am I called?* while on a flight in route to a developing country to help these people, well, maybe that was the answer to that question . . . at least for me, anyways.

CHAPTER NINE

THE BRIDGE SURVEY

I awoke the next morning to the sounds of a passing bus and a crowing rooster. Still half asleep, it took me just a moment to remember where I was. As I continued listening to the sounds outside, I glanced down and looked at the variety of bugs crawling on the floor. There were A LOT of bugs. When travelling, my number one "room rule" is that whatever gets placed on the floor, particularly suitcases, stays on the floor, and never gets placed on the bed.

Then I realized the meaning of a statement Mike had made to me after one of the mission team meetings, "Thomas, if a person isn't called to go . . . don't bring them." Suddenly, a big smile came on my face as I began to feel a sense of peace, reflecting back on the sign God had shown me on the airplane, and knowing, without a shadow of a doubt, this is where I was supposed to be.

Knowing I was called by God to build this bridge helped me quickly forget about the inconveniences of sleeping in a hot room and the morning's cold shower. I was thankful for the room to sleep in with electricity, the soft bed, the oscillatory fan, and the running water. The people who live in the stick homes built beside the road obviously had none of these modern luxuries.

After eating breakfast, we met with the *Alcaldía de Matiguas*, the Spanish name for the town governing body. This included the mayor and members of his council. Also attending the meeting were several community leaders. They represented the two communities whom the bridge would benefit.

It was standing room only as Mike and Danilo took charge of the meeting, explaining the plan to build a pedestrian walking bridge over the Bulbul River. Since I couldn't speak Spanish, I simply showed them several pictures of completed bridges I had printed from the Bridges to Prosperity website. Everyone became excited about the possibility of a bridge.

As we left the meeting, Mike gave me a quick summary—in English, of course. Basically, everyone was glad we were there and they fully supported our efforts. Then I asked Mike if he thought the town would be able to fund half of the money needed to buy the bridge materials. His answer was not what I had hoped for as he stated, "Thomas, the town doesn't have any money to contribute . . . our church will have to raise all the money needed for the bridge materials." The only good news I learned was that the town had a civil engineer, and he was at the meeting. This was exactly what this project needed to be successful, someone who could help me and B2P manage this bridge project from the ground.

The trip to the bridge site was down a long dirt road. The mountainous views were absolutely magnificent. The lady on the plane was right when she told me her country was very beautiful. But one thing I had already noticed: even though her people are poor, they are clean. Everyone I met was dressed well, in clean clothes, not filthy rags, like I would have imagined in a developing country. These people are proud of what they own, and take good care of it, whatever it may be.

The four-mile trip seemed longer than it was as we slowly made our way down to the river. It wasn't long before Oscar was stopping the van. This was it. Exiting the van, I saw a lot of people who were waiting for us. The mayor, his council, and the community leaders had arrived just ahead of us in another vehicle.

Everyone followed Mike down to the location of the proposed bridge, or at least the place he and the other mission team members had agreed almost two years ago. In preparation of our arrival, the community had cleared the larger brush, which allowed easy access for the group. As I looked across to the other side, I realized the enormity of this project. It was a long way across.

The gap reminded me of the Grand Canyon, especially since the other side appeared to be a thirty-foot rock wall. This was actually good . . . meaning the bridge foundation on that side would be built in stable rock well above the river. However, I could already tell the foundation location for this side was much lower and in questionable soil, but still appeared to be above the high water level of the river, which was marked on a large oak tree.

As everyone else talked, Avery approached me, smiling, and said, "OK, let's get started." Seeing she was holding her Abney Level, I sat down my backpack and first pulled out the two homemade survey rods, hoping she would be impressed with my ingenuity. She wasn't. But then I pulled out the Abney Level, and as I looked for the directions, she grabbed it and exclaimed, "This is a really nice Abney Level!"

Avery quickly explained to me how the instrument worked and the few simple steps to follow in using it to take angle measurements for the topographic survey. After she handed it back, I looked at all of the intricate parts of the small, fragile-looking instrument. A sight glass with a bubble-level mounted on top, and a movable protractor on the side to read the degrees.

I hadn't noticed, but the town's civil engineer, Nelson, was standing just behind me, listening. I wasn't sure if he had ever seen an Abney Level either, but between the two of us, I was confident we could figure it out. Thankfully, Avery was a patient person and showed me and Nelson how to read the degree scale while looking through the lens at a rock in the distance.

Then I remembered my friend in Blythewood had included several pocket-sized notebooks with the Abney Level, so I pulled those out. Avery explained these were to record the angle and distance measurements for each survey point, and to draw a rough sketch of the river's elevation profile. I had almost a dozen, so I gave her a few, since I knew I would never make use of them after this trip.

Nelson and I stood and perfected our use of the Abney Level, making sure we understood how to take correct measurements. After a few tries, the once strange little instrument became a very simple tool. We each took turns, choosing an arbitrary object, and then checking behind each other. Thankfully, Nelson knew enough English to where we could communicate with each other, since one person had to write down the distance and angle measurements.

By this time, I noticed Avery had walked to the edge of the river bank and was looking across, trying to determine the best location for the bridge's centerline. She had a roll of pink string in her hand, and gave it to Santos, the Gavilan community leader. For some reason, the community men looked confused.

Mike turned and explained to me this is a part of the river they don't normally cross, and they are afraid of disturbing a snake that may be hiding in the rocks near the river, or lying in the small debris near the river's edge. The rocks in the river bed sometimes have sharp edges, making the uncharted crossing even riskier. But the string had to take a straight path to the other side, which would mark the centerline of the suspended walking bridge. Finally, one older man stepped forward and volunteered to take the string.

As Nelson and I began taking the measurements we needed, I suddenly heard everyone start shouting, "Orlando!" We both rushed to where the others were gathered at the bank of the river. There, in the middle of the river, the man, not much over five feet tall, had apparently stepped in a hole. The water was almost up to his neck as he struggled to make his way out of the hole. Then some started laughing. But not once did he let go of the end of that string. *What determination*, I thought.

As he exited the river, Mike and the others met him to get the string. They had crossed the river further down, safely making their way on the large stones. Then I saw something amazing, the men scaling the face of the rock wall, grabbing whatever vine or crevice in the rocks they could find, just to get the string to the top of the cliff. And they did.

The string was cut and the ends secured around a tree on each side of the river, making for a visible bridge centerline. After this, Nelson and I finished taking the bridge's survey points, which included getting a good measurement of the bridge's span. It was slightly less than 60 meters, or 200 feet, which meant it was just within the Bridges to Prosperity's design criteria for using medium size cable anchors. Any longer would have meant a costlier design, and at this point, I knew we had to do everything we could to make this bridge more affordable.

That afternoon, everyone gathered in a close circle. The mayor of Matiguas spoke first, followed by a few of the community leaders. Mike was the last to speak to the group. I wished I knew more Spanish, because I couldn't understand a word that was said. But as several people began to pray, I knew they were asking for God's blessing for the bridge, while at the same time thanking Him for sending our mission team to them.

As we drove away, I started believing that the bridge project could actually be successful. But I still wasn't sure how we were going to raise the $25,000 needed to cover the cost of the construction materials, or even how long it would take for my church to raise that large sum of money. Then, I remembered Mike telling me not to worry, that the Lord would provide the money. How, I did not know. I could already sense this project becoming a test of my faith in seeing how God would provide the resources.

After supper, Nelson joined Avery and me at the small inn to go through the bridge design calculations. Within minutes of us sitting down, Avery had sketched out the bridge's profile. Then she began explaining how to calculate the required number of tiers for each side of the river, how to use the bridge survey information in calculating the height difference between the bridge towers, and the meanings of technical terms such as cable design sag, hoisting sag, free board, and low point. The calculations and civil engineering terms in the bridge design manual were now beginning to make more sense.

Trying to better explain cable sag and low point, Avery looked around for a piece of string. Finding nothing better to use, she grabbed her computer's electrical cord. She held one end and I held the other as she illustrated to Nelson why we needed to add an additional tier to the near-side foundation. She explained how the additional tier would shift the cable sag's low point more towards the middle of the bridge, meaning the bridge's weight would be more evenly shared by each foundation. This would also make the angles more equal for each cable passing over the cable towers.

The best single piece of information was the high water mark carved in the large oak tree, a mark resulting from flooding caused by Hurricane Mitch in 1998. This was needed to determine the bridge's freeboard, or bridge elevation above the flooded river. The design required that the freeboard be a minimum of two meters (about six feet) to allow for any large debris being washed downstream to safely pass underneath the bridge's walking platform.

Going through the design calculations the first time revealed we needed to add additional tiers to both sides to meet this design requirement. After re-doing these calculations, the bridge design would be basically finished. It was getting late, so I told Avery I would finish this later. But just knowing the proposed bridge site was an acceptable location by Avery was all I really needed to know.

Sitting in my room later that night, I felt really good about everything that had been accomplished at the bridge site that day. The bridge centerline was marked, the topographical survey was completed, and we had met with the community and town leaders at the bridge site. But then it occurred to me, Avery had agreed to meet with me on *her* free time, not her company's.

Now I realized why she had asked me to cover all of her expenses: this trip would have been out of her pocket, not Bridges to Prosperity's. And even though I had bought her plane ticket and was covering her meals, this didn't even come close to the appreciation I now felt I owed her. I'm not sure if I would have travelled to meet a complete stranger in a developing country, but she came on nothing but pure good will, because she is so passionate for what she does and genuinely loves the people these bridges help; a real heart of gold.

That Sunday morning as we all prepared to leave, I had written a personal thank you note to a new friend I had made, expressing my appreciation for all of their help. And as I went to seal the envelope, my eye caught sight of the Abney Level, and I remembered the blessing I had received from a friend in Blythewood, and how I wanted to pass that blessing on to someone else. I reached into my wallet and pulled out a one hundred-dollar bill and put it in with the note . . . for Avery. Sharing my loaf, that's what I enjoy doing more than anything else in life . . . priceless.

CHAPTER TEN

MY MOUNTAIN

During the flight to Nicaragua, God had revealed the physical sign, the "burning bush", I had prayed for. It was a clear sign that signaled me to take my other foot out of the boat and put it onto the water, and to commit my whole self to this project. Until then, for over forty years, I was simply enjoying being in the boat. Why?

Because for forty years, I never knew what it meant to really put God first. I mean, I said I was putting God first, but I didn't really know what I was saying. The real reason I never went to Nicaragua before this trip was my limited amount of vacation time, about which I said, "Lord, my vacation is for me and my family to enjoy." What God heard me saying was, "Lord, my vacation is for me and my family to enjoy, and NOT for You." Year after year, when the mission team would meet, I would say the same thing. Then, in December of 2008, noting my three full weeks of "banked" vacation on my pay stub, I remember thinking to myself, *Now what's your excuse going to be?*

My prayer was also answered concerning another mountain to climb. But it was a mountain I wasn't sure I was ready for, as Mike stopped me in the hallway at church the first Sunday in May and said, "Thomas, you have the heart and passion for this project. I want you to be in charge of getting the bridge designed, raising the funds however you feel led, and getting it built." But then he presented me with a seemingly impossible task, to raise the money by the end of the year so the bridge could be completed by May of 2011, so the community would not have to go through another winter having to wade across the river.

This was my mountain. Not only did I face the challenge of raising the $25,000 for the bridge materials (the amount required by the Bridges to Prosperity organization), but also the additional challenge of raising that amount in only eight months. Where would I start?

As the appointed project coordinator for the bridge, my first call was to Judy, the church's secretary. Finding out how much money was in the Nicaragua fund was an important starting point. I was surprised when she told me the fund had $5,770. She explained that when Mike introduced the pedestrian bridge project to the church in 2008, four church members made contributions totaling $4,500. This was a great start.

I spent the remainder of that week looking through all the information on the Bridges to Prosperity website, reading about the other communities where they had built a bridge. Then I came across their company brochure which had a Membership, Donations, and Renewals form. This form outlined the different levels of monetary contributions. For a $2,000 donation, a bridge would be dedicated in your name and a plaque placed on the bridge. A bridge would be named after someone giving a donation of $10,000. The website also listed gifts given "In Memory of" and "In Honor of" individuals. The idea of a bridge plaque was not something new, but maybe I could somehow combine the two ideas.

I needed a non-offensive way to challenge people to give a sizeable donation "In Memory of" or "In Honor of" an individual. But what amount? Even a $1,000 donation sounded too much to me. My dad had written me a $500 check to help with my trip expenses, but would others feel led to give that amount? And I knew not everyone would be able to give this much, but it would encourage those who could and at the same time allow them to give recognition to someone who had made a difference in their life. These names would be inscribed on a bridge plaque, just under the sentence, "This bridge is dedicated in the name of Jesus Christ."

Then I remembered, after talking with several church members after the worship service, it wasn't clear to them what type of bridge we wanted to build and why it was needed. So that afternoon, I wrote several paragraphs explaining the purpose of the bridge, why it was needed, and a brief summary of my trip to Nicaragua. I also included pictures taken at the bridge site and included a statement made that day, "This bridge is the dream of the people."

For two weeks, I worked on the bridge flier, each night adding a small detail or tweaking the layout. It had to look professionally done. After the final proofreading, I made one change to the title. To me and my church members, this was going to be a "Bridge to Faith," but to the community in Nicaragua, a "Bridge of Hope," a bridge that would greatly assist in meeting their basic needs during the rainy season. The new title better captured the attention of the humanitarian need.

I neatly packed as much information as I could on the bridge flier about the project and how to contribute. To me, this was a very important part of the fundraising because it was something my church members could easily share with their family and friends, either directly or by e-mail. And I knew in order to raise the $25,000 by the end of the year, this bridge flier needed to get into the hands of as many people as possible.

On Sunday, May 16th, I shared a brief bridge update with my church congregation. I had copies of the bridge flier for each member to take and read, and a lot of extra copies they could share with others. I told them it was my desire to share this mission project with other churches, and not just the big ones, but with the smaller congregation churches (like ours) that may not be able to support a mission project of this magnitude on their own. This was an opportunity for these churches to be a part of something big.

That week, I shared the bridge flier with friends who are members of very large churches in the Columbia area. I was encouraged as I learned that each church was already doing mission work in and around the city of Managua, the capital of Nicaragua. Another church was forming a mission team who would join with other churches in going to help rebuild churches and schools in earthquake-stricken Haiti.

I also shared the bridge flier with co-workers who attend churches in the town of Winnsboro, one of which my dad's sister, Aunt MeMe, attends. The response I received from her was that they support a mission team from their church which goes to Kentucky each year, and this was close to their heart.

To some, these may appear as closed doors of opportunities, but I know every church is filled with people having different talents and abilities. The Bible, in the book of Romans, states, "In Christ we are all one body," meaning no person's or church's mission work should ever be judged as having greater or lesser value than another's.

With this aside, I now felt the reassurance that my church, Sandy Level, was called by God to support and build the pedestrian bridge in Nicaragua. But even with the completion of the bridge flier and having shared the mission project with other churches, I knew these were only small steps, and that much bigger steps of faith would be required of me for this project.

CHAPTER ELEVEN

A Special Song

I now turned to sharing *The Faith Message* with other churches. I had already spoken to several friends about the possibility of their church supporting the mission project, giving them a packet which contained *The Faith Message* and ten bridge fliers. *The Faith Message* was a sermon I wrote in March to preach at other churches, challenging people to "step out of the boat" to help those in need, plant seeds, and support the bridge project with their prayers and donations.

Not surprisingly, the first church who invited me to come speak was my dad's church, Jones Crossroads Baptist, in Lancaster. This was my home church growing up. My parents had joined the church in the 1980's because that is where Mom's sister's family attended. It was a small, country church with a big heart with an outward expression of love for others. I remembered my mother each time I visited, always stopping to look at the beautiful granite church sign with the inscription at the bottom, "IN MEMORY OF JUANITA G. BLACK—1989." This was purchased with the memorials people had given in her memory.

I also shouldn't have been surprised when Dad called to tell me Aunt Jo was organizing a special dinner in my honor on the Wednesday night I would speak. In 1999, when Cynthia and I announced we would be moving to Blythewood, the church held an appreciation dinner for us. Aunt Jo was always so proud of me, for the family I was raising, and now for my involvement in this mission project. She often treated me more like a son than a nephew.

There was another person who was a big spiritual supporter in my life, Uncle Robert, my dad's brother. He was there at Jo and Bob's swimming pool when Dad, Mom, and I were all baptized. And he was there for me the night my mother passed away. Now, I wanted him to be there when I preached *The Faith Message* for the first time, so he could see the man I had become . . . a man who was following God's will in his life.

The week before I was to speak, I searched for a new song to sing during my sermon. Taking my son to school each morning gave me the opportunity to listen to several of my favorite Christian compact discs, which included the "WOW Hits 2010." The "WOW Hits 2010" was a double compact disc set I had gotten as a Christmas gift. I had previously performed two songs as solos, but wanted a new song to sing at my dad's church.

As I listened one morning, the song playing immediately grabbed my attention. The words went straight to my heart, and in my haste to find which compact disc track it was, I accidently hit the eject button. I quickly put it back in, and as the first song started, I was stunned. It was the first song on compact disc number one. All these months of listening to those two compact discs, and that song never before caught my attention like it did now. Maybe it never meant anything to me then, but now it did, only after fully surrendering my whole life to God and His purposes.

The song is "The Motions." I purchased the compact disc solo track and practiced it over a dozen times, each time its words becoming more and more powerful in their meaning. The song soon became a testimony to the changes that had occurred in my life in just the past few months. I planned to sing it near the end of *The Faith Message*, as an exclamation point to the message.

After finding the special song for the sermon, I worked hard to finish the tri-fold bridge display. In the center, I taped the map of Nicaragua I had purchased in the airport in April. On the map, I indicated the location of the bridge site. I surrounded the map with lots of pictures from my trip, including the meeting at the bridge site and the survey work.

Even after looking over this display, I realized some people would still see this project as a dream. At this point, I couldn't think of any words that would convince them otherwise. I placed one last picture on the tri-fold display. It was a picture of a finished bridge, spanning about the same distance as the one to be built in Nicaragua. I titled the picture "Bridge of Hope," and at the bottom placed a label of faith, "COMING SPRING 2011!"

CHAPTER TWELVE

THE FAITH MESSAGE

May 26th, 2010 is a date I will not soon forget. It wasn't because it was the Wednesday night I preached at my dad's church or that my Uncle Robert went with me; not for any of these reasons. It was the e-mail I received from Nelson, the civil engineer in Nicaragua, as I was starting to leave for Lancaster that night.

In his e-mail, Nelson explained days earlier, tropical storm Agatha had dumped a large amount of rain in the mountains, and the Bulbul River had flooded out of its banks. He included several pictures taken at the proposed bridge site; it was flooded. In fact, he noted the river was higher than in 1998, when Hurricane Mitch passed over Nicaragua. He also mentioned it had been several days since the communities could safely cross the river, and that it could be several more days before they could cross even on horseback. This information emphasized, without a doubt, the need for the bridge.

These images were fresh on my mind as I stood in the pulpit that Wednesday night at Jones Crossroads Baptist Church. I shared about my trip to Nicaragua, and followed by explaining the need for the walking bridge. After praying for God's blessing for the bridge project, I began the message.

Jesus Walks on the Water

"Immediately Jesus told his followers to get into the boat and go ahead of him across the lake. He stayed there to send the people home. After he had sent them away, he went by himself up into the hills to pray. It was late, and Jesus was there alone. By this time, the boat was already far away from land. It was being hit by waves, because the wind was blowing against it. Between three and six o-clock in the morning, Jesus came to them, walking on the water. When his followers saw him walking on the water, they were afraid. They said, 'It's a Ghost!' and cried

out in fear. But Jesus quickly spoke to them, 'Have courage! It is I. Do not be afraid.' Peter said, 'Lord, if it is really you, then command me to come to you on the water.' Jesus said, 'Come.' And Peter left the boat and walked on the water to Jesus. But when Peter saw the wind and the waves, he became afraid and began to sink. He shouted 'Lord, save me!' Immediately Jesus reached out his hand and caught Peter. Jesus said, 'Your faith is small. Why do you doubt?' After they got into the boat, the wind became calm. Then those who were in the boat worshiped Jesus and said, 'Truly you are the Son of God!'" Scripture: Matthew Chapter 14, Verses 22-33 NCV

When his followers saw Jesus walking on the water, they were all afraid. But one person, one believer, was willing to step out of the boat on his faith and go to Jesus . . . Peter. But as we look at this passage, it seems as if Peter was unsure at first, not fully trusting in his faith even after Jesus told them in the boat, "Have courage! It is I." Maybe Peter was placing one toe in the water when he said "Lord, if it is really you, then command me to come to you on the water." Peter was willing to go, but was unsure.

Jesus only called for one person to leave the boat, Peter: "Come." Why did Jesus do this? So Peter could test his faith; but Jesus already knew. Peter had to take the first step to get out of the boat; for him, a step of faith. But when Peter saw the wind and the waves, he became afraid. He started to sink, or doubt. Peter shouted, "Lord, save me!" Jesus reached out His hand and caught Peter, and took him back to the safety of the boat, where the other believers were. Faith is YOU taking the first step, with Jesus ready to take your hand and lead you the rest of the way.

We all are given different spiritual gifts. If you feel Jesus calling you to get out of the boat, you have to be willing to take the first step. If you feel the need to stay in the boat, then be ready to support the ones stepping out of the boat. Support them with your prayers, your monetary donations, and their family while they are away. Then when they come back into the boat, they will be ready to share their experiences with you, so your faith can also be strengthened.

Faith is being able to trust God, trusting fully in Him to take control of the circumstances. Faith is when asked to put your money where your mouth is, you follow through. Faith is before God pours out His blessings, He tells you to do something first, and you are willing to take that first step, even while doubting a little, just like Peter.

My Faith

When I was fifteen, I attended an Evangelistic healing crusade in Charlotte with my best friend, Jesse, and his dad. Sitting in the arena, I could barely hear the words to the songs. Over the past several summers, I had suffered with terrible ear infections. The doctor said it was from swimming in pools and the river too much. The only long term solution given by the doctor was to wear ear plugs to keep the water out. This solution seemed to work, until I went to the beach earlier that summer. I had forgotten my ear plugs, so I had no choice but to go into the pool without them. The result of my decision was an infection in each ear. They were infected and stopped up worse than ever.

During the service, Reverend Roberts asked everyone to fill out an information card. Besides all the general personal information, it asked me to write down one thing to be healed from, something physical. I put on my card, "God, please heal my ears." These cards were then collected by the ushers. I doubted anything would happen because as a relatively new Christian, my faith was not strong.

After Reverend Roberts' sermon came the healing part of the service. He stepped to the microphone and stated that everyone had filled out cards, many asking God for specific parts of their body to be healed. Then he explained that before God would heal your body, you had to demonstrate your faith. He said the ushers would be passing around offering plates in a few minutes. As I heard these words, I pulled out my wallet and took out three old one-dollar bills. They were right beside the twenty-dollar bill my dad had given me to buy something to eat.

As I waited for the offering plate to pass by, I barely heard Reverend Roberts speak these words: "If you want to be healed, you have to have faith; you have to plant a seed. To do that, I want you to reach into your wallet and pull out the largest bill you have—this represents your faith to God." As I looked down at those three one-dollar bills, something inside of me said, "Believe."

At that moment, I pulled my wallet back out and put those old one-dollar bills back in, and took out the new twenty-dollar bill. I held it firmly in my hand. Jesse saw what I had done, and asked, "What are you doing?" I replied, "I want my ears to be healed, and this is what he said I have to do." (Jesse's dad just looked over—didn't say a word. I'm not sure how strong their faith was, but I was testing mine—either with a miracle or a loss of $20.) As the offering plate passed, I placed my offering into it and silently prayed for the healing of my ears.

As Reverend Roberts began to pray, I could hardly hear him for the infection in my ears. Then he said, "By the power of the Holy Spirit, I command you to be HEALED," and then he loudly clapped his hands together. I literally felt the Spirit of God move over me, and immediately my ears were opened. "OH MY GOD," I exclaimed. Jesse looked over at me and asked, "What?" I replied, "I have been healed. I can hear everything so clearly now, like I haven't been able to in weeks!"

Now, I realize just because I have faith in a situation and want a miracle to happen, it may not. In this one instance in my life, it did. But many times we have to wait on the Lord; His timing and His will. It may even take years before we realize His blessing in a particular situation.

What about you?

What will your step of faith be? Maybe you're reading this and saying, "I know exactly what you're talking about, Thomas." While others may be saying, "I still don't understand what you mean by 'stepping out on faith.'"

Stepping out on faith may mean stepping out of the boat. Some may say, "If it's going to Nicaragua, then I'm not called to do that." But if not Nicaragua, then maybe a Mission Trip to Mississippi or Kentucky, even with another church. Ask your pastor to find out how you can join another church on its Mission Trip; by going it may change your life or the others you tell when you get back. But still others may say, "I feel more comfortable in the boat." That's alright, because Jesus only called one person out of the boat when he said to Peter, "Come." Everyone else stayed in the boat. But be prepared to support those that do step out of the boat.

But staying in the boat doesn't mean you can just stay in the middle of the stream, only looking straight ahead at the calm waters. Staying in the boat means you can still "build bridges," looking for opportunities to witness to people. Some will say, "I don't feel comfortable talking to people about Jesus." Then simply plant seeds, and let Jesus grow them. What do I mean by that statement? Pray that God will show you opportunities everyday where you can "step out on faith" and "build a bridge," trusting Him to take control of the circumstances.

Helping people who may be stranded on a rock, who need just a little bit of help—showing them a Christian cares. Ask God to show you the opportunities, and He will. The Lord will show you the person, the situation, and the need. He will put on your heart how to help them and how much.

But helping someone must be inspired and heartfelt, because if it's not, you will be doing it for the wrong reason. In the Bible, Jesus warns us of this when He says, *"Be careful! When you do good things, don't do them in front of people to be seen by them. If you do that, you will have no reward from your Father in heaven."* Scripture: Matthew Chapter 6, Verse 1 NCV

Your Money

Here's an example of planting seeds. When you're standing in line at the grocery store and you're the third person in line, you suddenly notice the cashier looking over the register tape, and a lady looking over her groceries—slowly pushing items to the side—items she did not have enough money to purchase. As she does, everyone in line become restless, because they are ready to get home to THEIR families—because it's Christmas Eve.

Then the lady behind you "steps out" on faith, trusting God to take over the circumstances. She approaches the cashier with a twenty-dollar bill and says, "I will pay the difference." And then she looks at the lady and says, "Merry Christmas." And as the cashier goes to hand this lady back her change, the lady then says, "Give that to her too." That's willing to be the one to "step out" and say, "Jesus, I will help her—I will build that bridge."

Now, what about the seed part? That's simple. This person just planted a seed in everyone's heart standing there that day, witnessing what just happened, so that next time they (including myself) may be willing to be the one to "step out" and help. If we plant the seeds, Jesus will grow them.

Imagine that you stop by the busy produce stand and purchase a bag of tomatoes for three dollars. As you get into your car, you notice an elderly man on a bicycle slowly passing by, looking over at all the new vegetables. Knowing your family will not eat all of those tomatoes, you pull up beside of him, let down your window and say, "Here, take this one." As he reaches in the window to take the tomato from your hand, he stares you straight in the eyes and whispers, "Thank you." At that moment you are so captivated that you can say nothing back, only stare into that man's watery eyes, because you can't believe what you just did, that you "stepped out" to help him, building a bridge to his need. As you drive off, you feel more blessed than he. Simple acts of kindness, that's what people need. Not the big things, just small, simple deeds.

Your Time

When the lady stands up in front of the church, and holds up her hands, showing everyone her physical disability, and says, "I cannot drive. I depend on someone else for everything—to take me to get the medicine

I need and to take me to my doctor appointments. And the one thing I now know, people will give you their money and people will give you their advice, but people will not give you their TIME."

When did you last "build a bridge" and give someone your time? Maybe you take the time to stop and help the person who has run out of gas. As you pass by, he holds up a gas can. So you stop, take the five-gallon gas can, and bring it back to him full of gas.

As you go to leave, he calls you an angel, because it's Sunday morning and no one else had stopped to help him—maybe because he wasn't wearing a suit, but an old T-shirt and cut-off blue jeans. Maybe because people didn't want to be late for their church service; but they're the ones who missed out on the true blessing, the true meaning of being a Christian.

"Then the King will say to the people on his right, 'Come, my Father has given you his blessing. Receive the kingdom God has prepared for you since the world was made. I was hungry, and you gave me food, I was thirsty, and you gave me something to drink, I was alone and away from home, and you invited me into your house. I was without clothes, and you gave me something to wear. I was sick, and you cared for me. I was in prison, and you visited me.' Then the good people will answer, 'Lord, when did we see you hungry and give you food, or thirsty and give you something to drink? When did we see you alone and away from home and invite you into our house? When did we see you without clothes and give you something to wear? When did we see you sick or in prison and care for you?' Then the King will answer, 'I tell you the truth, anything you did for even the least of my people here, you also did for me.'" Scripture: Matthew Chapter 25, Verses 34-40 NCV

Ken Frantz, the founder of Bridges to Prosperity, had shared this with me, "Building bridges not only help others cross, but demonstrates the power of the Cross."

Finally, a dear friend e-mailed me these words of encouragement, even as I searched out my own heart and purpose: "We all must remember that 'life' is a journey, not a destination, and as with any journey, Serving the Lord + loving people = purpose. AND we are all challenged to 'get out of the boat'—'move beyond comfort'—'love without limit'—that is where we'll discover not only who we truly are BUT the bounty of Christ."

After I finished speaking that night, I felt like I had taken another step. All had gone well: the dinner, the message, the new song, and Uncle Robert attending. Everything, with one exception . . . Aunt Jo wasn't there. Dad said she had not felt well all week and was very weak. This was a small disappointment to me, but I knew her thoughts and prayers had been with me.

CHAPTER THIRTEEN

It's Not About the Money

One month into the bridge fundraising campaign, and I could feel the momentum starting. Everyone could see the heartfelt passion I had for the bridge and the people who needed it. What no one knew was the bold statement I had made to these people before leaving Nicaragua in April.

The day after meeting with the community and its leaders at the bridge site, Mike got a phone call. It was Santos. He wanted to know when we were coming back to build the bridge. As Mike was explaining about having to raise the money for the materials, I boldly interrupted by saying, "Mike, tell him we'll be back next year to build his people a bridge."

To make good on my word, I knew the bridge flier needed to get into as many people's hands as possible. I confronted the church congregation and Deacons, challenging them to e-mail the bridge flier to every person they knew, sharing with others what God was doing through our church. For me, I'm all about the "one," meaning if one person reading the bridge flier made a donation or felt led to go and help build the bridge or minister to the Nicaraguan people, then my time spent editing and printing or e-mailing the flier would be well worth it.

Then, on Thursday, June 3rd, I received a phone call from Marie. She sounded very excited, telling me about having shared the bridge flier with the owner of her hair salon. Just Monday, she had come to my house to pick up her son, who had spent the afternoon studying for a test with my son. As she waited outside, I shared the details of my mission trip and gave her a bridge flier. She was simply amazed to learn how something we take for granted everyday, a bridge, can have such a big impact in the lives of the people in the mountain communities of Nicaragua.

I listened intently as she explained the hair salon's plan for a big open house event on June 14th. The purpose of the event was to promote the business and its new line of hair products. The festivities would include food, a raffle for hair products, a travelling salon tour bus, and a band. For three hours, the hair salon would give $10 hair cuts in not only the salon, but also ON THE BUS! The only stipulation was that all of the proceeds from the haircuts would go to a pre-selected charity or organization.

That's when Marie said she chimed in, telling the owner about a mission project they could choose to support. The owner said I needed to stop by and answer a few questions she had about the project. I thanked Marie four times for the seed she had planted, and told her the more I pray about this project, the more blessings seem to occur.

That day, I went by on my lunch hour and introduced myself to the hair salon's owner and answered her questions about the mission project. At that moment, she officially chose the Nicaraguan Bridge of Hope mission project to receive all the proceeds from the event. I was ecstatic. I would be allowed to set up a small table with the tri-fold bridge display I had shown at my dad's church. I could also hand out bridge fliers to customers as they entered the salon. She hoped to raise $500.

Unfortunately, the joyful feeling in my heart and the good news I had received that day quickly disappeared after answering one phone call that night. Dad called to tell me the news . . . Aunt Anne, his younger sister, had passed away. After suffering a stroke on Sunday, she was in the hospital slowly recovering, but her heart had become too weak.

This was a huge blow to me. Aunt Anne was in the hospital room with me and my dad the night my mom took her last breath, the night before Thanksgiving in 1989. And now, I would never have the opportunity to tell her about the bridge project I was involved with, and that my mother's name would be on the bridge plaque.

The next day, Cynthia and I went to visit with the family and share our condolences. I was outside sharing with Uncle Ernie, my dad's younger brother, details about the bridge project when Aunt MeMe, hearing what I was sharing, made a profound statement, "Yes, Tommy wants to build a bridge in Nicaragua, and now all he needs is the money." Though she was only stating a known fact, was that all people were hearing? I later thought more deeply about the meaning of her statement, and you know what . . . it was the truth. I was so caught up in meeting the financial need of the project, that the money part was all I was focusing on.

Then I remembered the discussion Mike and I had during a mission team meeting about the money for the project. I now understood what Mike was trying to tell me. To me, it was about who would give the money. To Mike, it was about faith, and letting God speak to people's hearts, and Him leading them to support the project, even telling them how much to give. For the project's financial need to be met, I simply needed to share with people the need for the bridge, and stop worrying about the money part. Even at that moment, I realized this project wasn't going to be only about building a bridge—but about FAITH.

The next night, I started typing the July Nicaragua Mission Team's Bridge of Hope project update. This is an excerpt from that update: *"Yes, to some, the Nicaraguan bridge project might only be about raising the money. I often find myself losing focus too. It's NOT about the money. It's not even about building a bridge. It's about growing relationships with other Christians, those on the mission team from our church and the Nicaraguan people; all working hand in hand, mixing concrete, laying stones, nailing the bridge planks in place, and then praising and thanking God for the given opportunity to do so. Yes, the money will be given and the bridge will be built, but will people's hearts be changed and will OUR walk with God be closer as a result?"*

CHAPTER FOURTEEN

A Special Prayer

The hair salon's open house on June 14th raised $465 for the bridge project, a direct result of one friend who shared a bridge flier with another friend. The bridge fund was now at $7,000.

On June 22nd, I completed the new bridge design calculations and submitted them to Bridges to Prosperity for their review. The revised design was based on the new high water mark set by tropical storm Agatha the previous month. This mark was almost one meter higher than the mark set by Hurricane Mitch in 1998. After reviewing the revised design myself, I realized the new freeboard was less than nine-tenths of a meter (about three feet), which was one meter less than the minimum design freeboard of two meters (about six feet). The freeboard is the distance between the bridge's walking platform and the river's highest level. This meant that during periods of extremely heavy rain, large debris could easily get caught underneath the walking platform, possibly damaging the walkway or the cables. This design shortfall needed to be addressed by the experienced team of engineers at Bridges to Prosperity.

With the design now finished, I finally had time to practice a song for the homecoming service at Jones Crossroads Baptist Church, which was the last Sunday in June. I was really busy, but saying no to Dad would have been really hard, especially with all the health issues he had overcome in the past year. I had chosen a new song, but decided on a favorite song at the last minute, "Cry Out to Jesus"—and I'm really glad I did.

Dad's church was packed that Sunday. I saw a lot of people I hadn't seen in many years; more importantly—Aunt Jo was there. She said she had been feeling a little better that week, and told me she made a special effort to attend because she loved her church family and homecoming meant a lot to her.

As I sang my song, with the words flowing from my heart, I could see Aunt Jo's face, gleaming with a big smile. Finishing and taking a seat behind her, she turned around and whispered, "Tommy, your mother would have been so proud of you; she is looking down from Heaven right now, smiling." I was not prepared for that comment, but knew her smile meant she was proud of me, too.

The next morning, I reflected back on Aunt Jo's words, trying to gain some level of satisfaction that I was doing all I could in terms of raising the money for the bridge. I had been stressed all day, had a headache, and was worried to tears about the bridge funds, the cost of the bridge, and seeing how much money still needed to be raised. It was now the end of June.

Then, stopping and sitting down for one minute and listening for His voice, this thought came to me, *When we've done all we can possibly do, and we still* see *the impossible, it's time to close our eyes . . . and pray.* That's it—plain and simple. And with that thought, I went and got down on my knees and said a special prayer for the bridge project, asking God to pour out His blessings on the upcoming fundraising events.

During the July Men's Ministry meeting, Mike discussed plans for the annual BLT (bacon, lettuce and tomato) sandwich fundraiser. This was always a good summertime fundraiser, because the tomatoes would be fresh out of people's gardens. It allowed people to come and enjoy a good BLT sandwich after Sunday's worship service and learn more about the mission team's upcoming projects in Nicaragua. This year, it was the bridge.

Then I mentioned to the men about having a car wash fundraiser in August or September, since the youth mission team raised over $500 at theirs. This would give the Blythewood community itself an opportunity to support the bridge project. The idea got some general discussion before we moved on to other business.

During the worship service that Sunday, I gave the monthly bridge update to the church congregation. These updates always included my testimony, a story to challenge each person to give, and an update on the fundraising. This month I announced the date for the BLT luncheon—July 18th, and also explained in more detail the concept of the bridge plaque. I was excited to share that the bridge project was now officially listed on the Bridges to Prosperity website. In fact, it was the first bridge project listed for Nicaragua, even though other sites had been surveyed by the B2P engineers.

Then Mike got up to speak. He shared a unique fundraising idea I'm not sure anyone had ever heard of before. He simply stated, "Thomas wants your money, but I want your junk!" Basically, people needed to look around their yard for old lawnmowers, junked cars, worn out farm equipment, or anything else made of metal that could be hauled to the scrap yard, where the average salvage value was at seven cents per pound. It seemed almost like "free" money. I was so impressed with the novelty of the idea that I gave the fundraiser an official name, "Metal to Money."

The following Sunday was the BLT fundraiser luncheon. During the luncheon, I showed a short presentation with pictures from the proposed bridge site, the existing crossing location, and the flooded river in May. I gave a broad overview of the project details and answered people's questions about the project. I made sure everyone understood that all of the money would be used to purchase the bridge materials. I encouraged everyone to take extra copies of the bridge flier to share with their family and friends.

I called our church secretary, Judy, that Tuesday to find out how much money had been raised at the BLT luncheon, and I was shocked—$3,276. And then she told me that in the weeks prior, four other $500 donations had been given, each with the paperwork filled out for the bridge plaque. Members *had* wrapped their heart around the bridge project. These donations, when added with those from the luncheon, brought the bridge fund to $13,000. We were now over halfway to reaching the set goal.

That night, I got a phone call from Jessica, one of the church members. I thought she was simply calling to make sure I had reserved the animals for the outdoor live nativity, but that wasn't it. Her call was about the BLT fundraiser. She said as she sat and listened to me talk about the community and the bridge, she felt God calling her to go to Nicaragua. At first she wasn't sure, because she had never even flown on an airplane and had a real fear of flying. But after she took a bridge flier home and carefully read back over it, she knew God was calling her to go. I expressed my joy in her acceptance to follow her heart and God's calling on her life. Knowing one person was stepping out of the boat because of the bridge project was a real blessing to me.

Less than three months after getting back from Nicaragua, I realized this project had already taught me so much, not just about other people, but about myself. I could feel my faith muscle being strengthened with each step of the journey. But for some reason, God wasn't through testing me.

It always seemed that in my life, when things were going good, something would happen to make me stop and question my faith. And the phone call I received from my dad on Saturday, July 24th, telling me that Aunt Jo had passed away would be no different. After spending a week in the hospital, in need of a heart valve replacement, she had become too weak and was sent home to spend her last days with her family by her side.

When Cynthia and I went to see her that Friday evening at her home, she was too weak then to open her eyes and acknowledge our voices. Even though I had prepared myself for this, it still hit me hard, remembering how much she thought about me. At that moment, I could feel myself starting to slide back down the mountain, but knew I had to keep looking up, keep trusting in God, and climb.

CHAPTER FIFTEEN

THE STORIES HE GAVE ME

The first week in August was my family's annual beach trip, which gave me a chance to slow down and reflect back on the past three months. I had preached *The Faith Message*, given two project updates, and helped with two fundraisers. But deep down, I felt the need to be sharing more of the stories I was told while in Nicaragua. After all, this IS what Jesus told me to do in my vision, when He said, ". . . start telling the stories I will give to you . . ." But how?

The church newsletter was one way. Though I had never written anything for the newsletter before, it would be a great way to share these stories. But would the stories encourage people to support the bridge project? That would be for them to decide; I only needed to do my part.

Each morning that week, I prayed for God to give me the words to type—the story to share and the challenge for His people. And He did! Sitting at the computer each morning, I could feel the words flowing from my heart onto the keyboard.

The August newsletter article was titled, "Build a Bridge—Give Your Time." It started with thanking those who had helped with the BLT luncheon and stating that $3,276 was raised for the bridge. Then I shared a story of when someone gave their time by stopping to help a man who needed gas on a Sunday morning, demonstrating a simple act of kindness. I challenged others to do the same, because that's what people need in this world. I stated that the bridge project is a simple deed, but it, too, is more about building relationships with the Nicaraguan people.

The September newsletter article, titled "Build a Bridge—The Whole Story," was an expansion of the story in the August newsletter. I shared all of the story's details, including the fact that it was me who had stopped to help the man. Then I asked a challenging question, "Will you stop and help by giving to the Build-a-Bridge fund?"

The October newsletter article was titled, "Build a Bridge—The End Pieces." Here, I told about the end pieces of the bread, the ones that are often unevenly cut or thin that get discarded—thrown away. The end pieces reminded me of the Nicaraguan communities who need the bridge, people no one else has stopped to help. Then a challenging statement, "Let's reach in and take them by the hand, and share our loaf with them."

The November newsletter article told the story of two children who had survived an attack by a hive of killer bees. It emphasized the fact of how almost everyone thought they were dead, but because of faith and prayer, they, in fact, survived. I titled the article, "Build a Bridge—A Raised Hand," because that was the sign the firemen wanted to see before they would go in and attempt to save the children, for each child to raise a hand. Then the challenge—the people who have drowned in the river, they are raising their hand once again, but this time not to be saved from the river, but for someone to come and build their children a safe way to cross it.

The December newsletter article was a play on words, "Build a Bridge—It's Not Just a Bridge." It started by telling the story of a little girl losing one of her flip-flops in the river, and then risking her life to retrieve it. Then a fact of how the bridge will give the people a sense of pride like they have never known, because they will no longer have to change out of their wet clothes to dry ones to attend school or go to work. It's not just a bridge.

For the first time, I began to see how God was "moving" through the bridge project. More importantly, I could feel the Holy Spirit moving in my own heart, drawing me even closer to God. It was now my prayer, not that the bridge would be built, but that people's hearts be changed, and that everyone's walk with God be closer as a result of the bridge project.

CHAPTER SIXTEEN

The Car Wash Fundraiser

By September, the Build-a-Bridge fundraising campaign had surpassed $18,500 in donations. The bridge plaque was filling up with names, the bridge's newsletter story for the next five months were written, and I was preparing to give one final update on September 26th to the church congregation.

September 18th was the day of the Bridge of Hope donation car wash. Sunday's church bulletin had included the date and time of the car wash, as well as a request for "washers." I had also sent an e-mail to the church's Men's Ministry, reminding them of the need for volunteers and to tell their friends—so there would be plenty of cars to wash.

I chose to meet and setup for the car wash in Blythewood at 8:00 a.m., early enough to solicit vacationers departing from the two adjacent hotels. There was also a baseball tournament in Blythewood and a Women's Ministry event at my church that day, meaning more potential customers. My faith goal that Saturday was to raise $1,000, which would bring the bridge's fundraising total close to $20,000. I had it all planned out.

I got an early start that morning by helping Cynthia get coolers filled with ice for the baseball tournament. I was running slightly behind schedule when my cell phone rang—it was Jessica. She wanted to know where I was, since I had told everyone to meet at 8:00 a.m. After my initial shock, I jokingly told her that I had announced that time so *I* would be there by 8:15 a.m., and I didn't expect anyone to actually be there at 8:00 a.m. I assured her that I was on my way with the buckets, soap, and hoses. Now feeling a bit worried, I asked her how many others where there waiting on me. I was relieved, at least at that moment, when she replied, "No one."

As I drove into the gas station's parking lot, I noticed a lot of cars had already parked in the spaces where I wanted to set up the car wash. Several of the cars apparently belonged to people who had carpooled to work that morning, since their owners were nowhere to be found. Regardless, I was a bit discouraged, since this meant we would now have to set up the car wash in the rear of the parking lot, which wouldn't be as visible to the passing public. My discouragement grew greater when, after Jessica and I had finished filling the eight wash buckets with soap and water, and stretched out the three water hoses, no one else had shown up to help. It was 8:30 a.m. Then, I suddenly found myself saying a short, simple prayer, "Lord, we have provided the buckets of soap, now I pray for You to provide the hands and the cars."

Meanwhile, at the Blythewood baseball field, one friend had already asked Cynthia where I was, since I had never missed any of my son's baseball games. Cynthia simply replied, "He's at the Nicaraguan bridge car wash fundraiser."

"Really?" said my friend, "I need to go and get my truck washed . . . I owe him." Cynthia immediately knew what she meant, but anyone else overhearing their conversation might not have fully understood the meaning in Jeannie's response. For Jeannie, it was a supportive way to pay back the generosity I had shown to her and her husband, Richard, in his hospital room in April.

Just before noon, I saw Jeannie and Richard's truck pulling into the car wash. They had also brought their son, my son, and another teammate. From the car wash, the three boys walked up to Blythewood Road, where I was holding a large sign with the words, "Bridge of Hope—Nicaraguan Mission Project—Donation Car Wash." For some reason, I seemed to be having a difficult time getting people to stop and get their car washed.

Needing a break, and seeing the boys really wanted to be everyone's center of attention, I let them hold the sign. As I walked to find a spot in the shade, I noticed Mike, my church's mission team leader, walking over from the car wash. Mike was always cracking jokes, so I wasn't sure what he could possibly conjure up to say about the car wash. But today, for some reason, he had a more serious look on his face.

Walking up, Mike looked me straight in the eyes and asked, "Thomas, have you heard what happened at the bridge site this week?" Pausing briefly, trying to read more into his question, I replied, "No, I haven't." He continued, "Do you remember the older man who took Avery's string across the river to mark the centerline of the bridge?" I thought for a moment, but drew a blank stare.

Seeing I couldn't remember, Mike explained, "He was the one who, as he got towards the middle of the river, slipped into a hole, and everyone laughed. His name was Orlando." The moment Mike said his name I remembered the incident, because after he slipped, he struggled to regain his footing in the river. Then, after seeing he was safe, the people all laughed and hollered his name, "Orlando," at which time I immediately thought of Orlando, Florida.

Mike, pausing briefly, stated, "Thomas . . . he drowned in the river this week." At that moment, I just stood there—looking at Mike with disbelief—frozen, as his words sank into my heart. I slowly turned and stared over at the car wash, at the workers, and at the few cars that were being washed. I remembered thinking, *Oh God, why? Why did You allow this to happen on my watch? Why did You allow me to come this far, only to fall short?*

Never in my life had I given so much of not only my time, but my heart, in supporting a mission project. As I continued staring at the car wash, I became angry. But not at God, at myself, because I felt like I hadn't done enough to raise the money for the bridge. To me, raising the money was now a personal vendetta, and I didn't care what I had to do or say to raise the rest.

After a few minutes, I turned back to Mike and asked him what had happened. Mike explained, "The rains had been heavy, and the people had not been able to cross the Bulbul River for several days. Orlando had an old dug-out canoe, and needed to sell his corn—corn he could sell in the town of Matiguas for money to buy food and supplies for his family. There were others who also needed to get to town, so he let them ride in the canoe with his corn. As Orlando struggled to maneuver the canoe filled with people and his corn in the high water of the Greater Matagalpa River, it began to take on water. Everyone else left the canoe and made it safely to shore, but Orlando stayed in the canoe. He drowned trying to save not only his corn, but the canoe."

I just stood there, speechless; absolutely speechless. We were so close to building him and his people a bridge. Mike broke into my thoughts by asking how much money we had raised to-date. I told him we were at $18,500, and that our congregation and others had already given so much.

As Mike was walking away, Jeannie and Richard drove up in their freshly-washed truck. They had come to get the boys and take them back to the baseball field for the next game. Richard looked to be doing well, considering the serious neck injury he had received, a result from the motorcycle accident in April. Though his neck still appeared to be a little stiff, at least he was walking. As I continued talking with them, I asked

Jeannie if she had gotten a bridge flier. She said she had, but was going to wait and read it at home later that night. So I quickly shared with them a few of the project's details and thanked them for coming to support the fundraiser.

That night as I counted the donations from the car wash, it seemed like a good amount. But when added to the running total, only put us at $19,000. Then the thought raced through my mind, not as a prayer, but only as a thought, *Lord, people have given so much, and we are so close to the goal, but I'm just not sure how much more people are going to be able to give.*

Sunday was the last day of the baseball tournament. Later at home that night, Cynthia told me I needed to call Jeannie. Cynthia said Jeannie had read the bridge flier she had received from the car wash, and wanted more information. Being the project coordinator, I was always eager to share more details concerning the need for the bridge.

I was a little nervous calling Jeannie, not exactly sure what questions she would have, so when she answered the phone, I let her do most of the talking. She told me, after reading the bridge flier, she was really touched by the need for the bridge, and had no idea people in developing countries often risked their lives to cross a river for their food and basic necessities. It also touched her that there were grown adults, not children, washing cars on a hot Saturday morning. This really impressed upon her heart how much this mission project must mean to our church. She went on to say she had shared the bridge flier with her pastor at church that morning, and he asked her to get more information about the project.

I told her that I appreciated her comments, and was glad Richard had recovered so well from the motorcycle accident. I also thanked her for coming to the car wash to support the bridge project, even though I had told them they never had to repay me for what I gave them.

She continued the conversation by telling me that Richard was so moved that someone from the baseball field would have taken their time to come to the hospital to see him. She said that I seemed to be doing well financially, and most people in that position stop associating with the lower class, and only start thinking about themselves and their "stuff," but I still seemed like an ordinary person who cared about people. Then when she found out I was the project manager for the bridge project, she felt the Lord at the car wash saying, "Give back to him."

As I continued listening, Jeannie told me something that at first I didn't understand. She said her church had met for the last time that morning, and a small group from their church was meeting on Wednesday night to divide up the building fund: to support missionaries in Japan, research on breast cancer, food pantries, and other suggested charitable organizations. She felt led to present the bridge project to the group and ask for money to help with its fundraising. She asked me how much money we had raised, and how much more we needed.

My response to her was somewhat delayed, because I was totally surprised and overjoyed that she would even consider doing that. I told her my church had raised $19,000, which included the $515 from Saturday's car wash. I told her about the Bridges to Prosperity organization and their requirement of having $25,000 upfront to cover the cost for the bridge materials. My church needed to raise $6000 more by the end of the year, so the construction could be started and the bridge completed before the rainy season began, which is normally during the month of May.

I told her I had to give a bridge update to my church congregation next Sunday, and I wasn't sure what I was going to say except for them to give more money. I told her of my prayers for other churches to become involved in the bridge project and the fundraising. Then I told her about Orlando drowning last week in the river, below where the bridge was planned to be built. I told her the whole story—then, for a moment, we both cried together.

I promised to e-mail her pastor more information about the bridge, including *The Faith Message* and the previous bridge update I had given. Before hanging up, I told her that if her church even gave $1,000, that would put us at $20,000, and that maybe my church congregation would give a little more, seeing how close we were to reaching the $25,000 goal.

After I hung up the phone, I told Cynthia what Jeannie and I had talked about. Cynthia was just as surprised and wanted to know more about Jeannie's church. I told her Jeannie's church was part of the John Wesleyan church organization, and that several years ago, the church administrator had come down from Greenville to close all the smaller Wesleyan churches around Columbia and make those congregations join a big mega-church the organization had built in Columbia. But Jeannie and her church wanted to stay the small "lighthouse" church in the community and wanted to build their own meeting place. After only three years, the membership had continually declined because members began to join other churches. Last Sunday, her pastor, seeing that the vision of building a meeting place of their own was seemingly out of reach, suggested to the remaining members that the church's building fund be divided up, so missionaries and local charitable organizations could be helped now.

That night, I thought back on my phone conversation with Jeannie. Could this be God's answer to my prayer for another church to become involved in the project? I had searched out all the larger churches in the Columbia area, knowing they would have a large membership who could more easily support the fundraising efforts than a smaller church congregation. But now, surprisingly, here was a friend who was willing to ask her church to support the bridge project—a church that was basically closing its doors because of its declining membership. Then I began to ponder how much they would give, if anything at all. After all, these people had never heard of this project and were not even part of the same church denomination as my church. Would they support a Baptist church's mission project? All I could do was pray that they would.

CHAPTER SEVENTEEN

AN INCREDIBLE STORY

On Monday, I attended the Mission and Ministry Team meeting at church to begin planning for the annual drive-thru living nativity. At the meeting, I briefly mentioned that a friend's church was meeting on Wednesday night to divide their building fund between foreign missionaries and other charitable organizations, and that my friend, Jeannie, was going to recommend they make a donation to support the Bridge of Hope mission project. Jessica was excited, since she remembered giving Jeannie the bridge flier at the car wash on Saturday.

After our meeting, I stopped Pastor Ben in the hallway and told him the story of the ten one-dollar bills. This was the reason Jeannie and Richard had come to the car wash on Saturday, simply to repay the generosity I had shown to them in April. Then, I made a profound statement, "Ben, if Jeannie's church gives $1000 because I had given them ten $1 bills, wouldn't that be a modern day version of the multiplying of the fish in the Bible?" Pausing briefly, Pastor Ben exclaimed, "Thomas, it would be an incredible story!"

That night I went home and typed two pages of notes and my thoughts for Sunday's bridge update, thanking people who came out to help wash cars, telling of how much money was raised, Jeannie's church's willingness to help support the mission project, and the drowning of Orlando. Finally, I challenged people to open up their hearts and to give so we could reach the fundraising goal of $25,000, telling them that whatever they had already given, they needed to give that much again. Maybe that was too bold, but it was getting late, and I knew I could put the finishing touches on it the next night.

On Tuesday morning, I typed Pastor Ben an expressive e-mail.

September 21, 2010

Pastor Ben,

I finally realized why this bridge project has been such an emotional up and down journey for me—I put too much faith in "man" and not God. I expect other people to want to give as much as I do when they say, "I want to give," but then do not. Or I expect too much, like with Jeannie and her church, expecting them to wrap their heart around this project and say, "We'll make up the difference," getting my hopes up, only to be disappointed. Ben, I'm tired of being disappointed. I want God to show Himself, and for the end of the fundraising to be a great awakening. But that's what I want, for the fundraising to wrap up with a miracle gift, something totally unexpected—for people to say, "Wow!" So I will pray for His will to be done, and not my own. And if it happens, know it was He who allowed it to . . . and not something I had hoped for. But it would make a great story, oh my, wouldn't it."

Thomas

That Tuesday night, I sat down at the computer and read back over the two pages of notes I had typed the night before. I stared at all of those words for over twenty minutes, but each time when I read them, they made no sense at all—none. Then, I got up and emptied the kitchen trash, and as I was coming up the steps from the garage, I stopped and said, "Lord, give me the words You would have me to say."

I came in the house, sat back down at the computer, and started typing at the top of the page. I ended up deleting every bit of what I had typed the previous night. I stopped the bridge update for Sunday with the last two sentences from the e-mail I had sent my pastor that morning, "So I will pray for His will to be done, and not my own. And if it happens, know it was He who allowed it to . . . and not something I had hoped for." When I had finished typing those two sentences, I sat back and thought to myself, *Now, I just have to wait until tomorrow night and find out how much Jeannie's church gives.* Then I heard His voice, "Finish it now." Not even pausing to think, I typed these words, "And you know what . . . HE DID!" As I stared at those last few words, I remember asking myself, *Did what?*

It was now 11:35 p.m. I knew Ken Frantz wouldn't be up this late, but I wanted to share with him the bridge update for Sunday and remind him to say one final prayer that Jeannie's church would vote to support the bridge project. In fact, I still have that e-mail, and in the last sentence, I wrote, "Say a prayer, and expect a miracle to happen with this project, my friend." So I was shocked when I got Ken's reply at 12:06 a.m. Ken must have been praying at the same time I was typing my e-mail to him, as his e-mail reply read, "Thomas . . . you are amazing. I prayed for your success, and just came up from prayer for you and the village in Nicaragua with a big smile on my face—a sign?"

Wednesday was a busy day at work. I was on the phone all morning, and hadn't even had time to turn on the radio, which sits on the small window shelf behind my desk. The window blinds were fully closed because the morning sun was so bright. When I turned around from my desk, I looked up and noticed something I had never noticed before in my office window: a cross. I stopped for a moment before realizing it was formed by the light filtering in through the window frame. Still, it was like the Lord was saying, "I am here. Now you do what you know how to do (pray), and I will do what I know how to do (a miracle). Stop worrying, I WILL make up the difference." At that moment, I said a prayer, and let go of all the worrying I had about the money.

That night during choir practice, Cynthia sent me an e-mail, "JEANNIE IS CALLING YOU . . . TAKE THE CALL!!!!" I quickly exited the choir, put up my music folder, and waited for Jeannie's call. Minutes passed like hours. Finally, my phone rang . . . it was Jeannie.

We talked for probably thirty minutes. I shared with her the story of the ten one-dollar bills and what they meant to me in my life, but I wasn't sure what they had meant to her. Then, she said just before I came that evening to visit Richard in the hospital, her son Jacob had asked her for a dollar so he could buy a drink. When she looked in her pocketbook, she didn't have any change. She told him he would have to wait. Then when I gave her that card, and after she opened it, and all those dollars were lying in her lap—she almost cried. She felt such a blessing was given to her, by someone from the baseball field—not even a family member.

I told her when I left the hospital that night I was thinking, *These people are going to think I'm crazy and weird—who would do something like this?* She boldly interrupted, "Thomas, No! You never know how what you give will affect other people, and NEVER worry about what people think about what you do for them. You don't know what people are going through." Then the thought occurred to me, *The statement I keep telling people in the church updates and newsletter stories is absolutely true,* "In life, it's not the big things people need, but small, simple acts of kindness."

Before I let her continue, I needed to confront her with something. "Jeannie," I started out, "I talked with Jessica after we talked on Sunday night, and told her the exciting news that a couple from the baseball field had gotten their truck washed Saturday, and were going to recommend that their church make a donation to the bridge project. Jessica remembered you because you had brought Jordan and Shawn to the car wash, who were still in their baseball uniforms. I told Jessica you had gotten a bridge flier and were really touched at the need for the bridge. Then Jessica told me when she first offered you a bridge flier, you told her that you didn't need one, and then you turned around to leave. Jessica was shocked that someone wouldn't want a flier."

After a brief pause, Jeannie answered, "Yes, I remember after I paid her, she did offer me a flier. I told her I didn't need one, but when I turned to walk away, a thought came in my mind. I turned back and said, 'Yes, give me one of those . . . I have someone I want to share it with.'"

At that moment, I quickly realized how close Jeannie came to not taking a bridge flier—for none of this even happening right now. As I thought back to that Saturday, I realized her truck was getting washed at the exact same time Mike was telling me the news of Orlando's drowning. God WAS there that day. It wasn't *just* a car wash.

She continued our conversation by saying she had started to go into her church's meeting and tell the others what I meant to her, and that they needed to support this project. But she didn't have to, because her pastor brought up the bridge project on his own, sharing with the group from the information I had sent. He told them this was one of the greatest mission projects he had ever heard of, and recommended they fully support it. The members' "yes vote" was unanimous. At that point I was overwhelmed, even before she shared the amount they would be donating.

That night as Cynthia and I talked about Jeannie's church, she made a stunning statement, "Thomas . . . Jeannie's church . . . the money in their building fund . . . that represented their dream . . . their dream of one day building their own church. They are giving up THEIR dream to support OUR dream." Wow, I hadn't thought about it in that way, but she was right. During the project update on Sunday, I would be sure to remind my church's congregation of that fact.

And that Sunday, as I stood in front of my congregation giving the bridge update, I could barely hold in all of the emotions that were flowing through my body. To me, Jeannie's church supporting the bridge project was the answer to my prayer for another church to become involved and support the bridge project, even if only in a small way. And now, I fully understood what the words I had typed on Tuesday night meant, and those would be the last two words of my update.

After talking for over ten minutes, which included sharing the story of Orlando, the car wash fundraiser, and of Jeannie's church making a donation to the bridge fund, the congregation probably thought the words, "Stop worrying, I WILL make up the difference," was just a faith statement to end the update. But I had the answer, as I continued, "And you know what . . . HE DID!" At that moment, there was complete silence as everyone stared at me. Then I broke the silence with these words, "And THEY DID . . . Jeannie's church voted to give $6,000 to the Nicaraguan bridge project! The fundraising is finished!" After hearing those words, I could see the astonishment on everyone's faces.

At the end of the service, Pastor Ben asked me to stand at the front of the sanctuary so everyone could come by and speak, just to show their appreciation for my dedication to the bridge project. As the last few members were coming up to me, I saw Jessica as she hurriedly came down the aisle towards me.

"Thomas, you are not going to believe this, but a couple was so moved at everything that happened in the service today, they are going to pay for my entire trip next year to Nicaragua!" "That's great," I said. Maybe not sensing enough excitement in my reply, she said, "No, but you don't understand. I've been working a second job cleaning people's houses to save enough money to buy my plane ticket. Now I can use that money to buy things for the children in Nicaragua!" After hearing her explanation, I fully shared in her excitement. I saw the personal sacrifices she was making for the trip. She had now received her blessing from God for being so faithful to His church, for being the first person at the car wash that Saturday morning, and for handing out the bridge fliers.

Then it occurred to me. The small congregation church—literally closing its doors—crossing denominational boundaries—seeing this as God's project, and not man's—giving up their dream of one day building a permanent meeting place, all so that the Gavilan and Patastule communities in Nicaragua could realize their dream of a bridge. Then dividing up their building fund—voting to give $6,000 to the Bridge of Hope, which meant the fundraising goal would be met in only five months! Yes, the small congregation church sacrificially gave the most, just like the poor widow in the Bible who gave all she had to live on. (Mark Chapter 12, Verses 41-44 NCV)

Yes, that ONE car wash fundraiser, that ONE second in time, that ONE bridge flier, that ONE Saturday morning, my ONE prayer for another church to become involved in the fundraising efforts. My ONE prayer that morning for God to bless a simple car wash fundraiser, and then ONE friend coming to the car wash because of ten one-dollar bills I had given to her and her husband in a hospital room in April—only because someone had done the same for me over twenty years ago. God showed Himself, not secretly, but for everyone to see, and now for everyone to read about.

All the "Why did this happen to me?" questions in life are not always known at the time—some answers and blessings may take months for one to realize, some years, and yes, for me, twenty years. Everything in life has a reason and a purpose, absolutely everything. God has a purpose for each of our lives—someone to witness to, someone to reach out and help, someone to be a friend to—all we need to do is slow down enough, be still, and listen for His voice to simply tell us "who."

Ten one-dollar bills, seemingly insignificant to me twenty years ago, planted a seed in my heart that would continue to grow, then God telling me when to share and exactly who to share it with. Now, I'm able to share that blessing with two communities in Nicaragua who need a bridge, so no one else has to drown in that river. *Thank You Lord, Thank You!*

Author's Comments: I know this almost seems like a made-up story, one found in a fairy tale—happening in a faraway land. But the story is true. I should know, because I was there—first on the receiving end of ten one-dollar bills, and then on the giving end. And now, if I ever feel led to share my faith with someone, I simply start out the conversation by asking them this simple question, "Would you like to hear an amazing true story?"

CHAPTER EIGHTEEN

MEETING WITH THE *ALCALDÍA*

The bridge fundraising was one of the most incredible journeys I had ever taken. I told Cynthia this was one of the greatest stories of God's grace and blessing I had ever personally experienced. More importantly, I had grown in my faith.

I was serious when I told people that I was so blessed and fulfilled by the fundraising that I didn't even need to go and build the bridge. But although the bridge fundraising had been an incredible experience, I still knew there was one more mountain I had to climb . . . to actually go and build the bridge. So on February 4th, 2011, Mike and I boarded a plane to go and do just that.

We arrived in Nicaragua late that Friday evening. Even though it had been almost a year since I had last set foot in the country, the sights and sounds made it seem like only a month. Once you see people living in extreme poverty along the roadside, the pictures your mind takes become etched into your memory. The sight of these people quickly reminded me of why I had come back—to help the people in two mountain communities build a bridge to a better life.

We spent that Friday night in Managua and got an early start the next morning to travel to Matiguas. As we made our way through the crowded streets of Managua, I was sure to take in all the sites along the way—the men and women standing in the middle of the street, waiting for the light to turn red, selling small plastic bags of water, hand-made jewelry, cell phone chargers, vegetables, and fresh baked breads. Tables lined one side of the street as far as one could see, with people selling everything from name brand shoes to pocketbooks. This is the way of life for these people—hoping enough people will stop so they can earn enough money to provide food for their family.

Still, these people have a job, making life a little better than the people living in the communities where the bridge will be built. For the people in the mountain communities, they rely solely on being able to cross a river everyday to carry canisters filled with fresh milk to the collection location, or to get to their farmland and cattle. When the rain pours down and the river floods, it affects their whole livelihood. To me, this is what makes the bridge project so rewarding, so fulfilling: it will help improve the lives of two whole communities.

As we continued to travel farther up into the mountains, the anticipation began to get the better of me. Milosz with Bridges to Prosperity had last e-mailed me in January, telling me the bridge construction had begun. I knew the foundations for the large bridge tiers would need to be excavated first, with all of the digging done by hand. I was anxious to see how much the communities had accomplished over the past three weeks.

Without the aid of a backhoe, the Gavilan and Patastule communities would have had to form work teams to dig out the foundation for the bridge tier on each side of the river. Then I remembered the large amount of rock at the location of the farthest foundation, which would make the digging on that side even more difficult, if not impossible. Two questions then came to mind: *Would the required amount of manual labor prove too difficult, and if so, would they get discouraged and quit?* I knew in my heart that if the answer to either of these questions was "yes," then my church's fundraising efforts would have been for naught.

The three hour trip to the town of Matiguas seemed like seven. As we turned on the dirt road leading to the river, I could slowly feel my heart rate speeding up ever so slightly. Then I saw the Bulbul River. At that moment I remembered Orlando, who tragically lost his life in the Greater Matagalpa River. He was a family man who shared the same vision for the bridge as my church family. The only thought that brought any comfort to me was that if every time someone walked across on the bridge, they would wonder why Orlando's name was included on the bridge plaque. Then someone would share the story of Orlando's unselfish efforts in helping with the initial survey for the bridge in 2010. It was a fitting tribute to his life.

Walking down to the location for the bridge, I noticed two large piles of stones the communities had already gathered. At a quick glance, I could already tell a lot more of the larger stones would be needed for the construction. The two communities had worked hard preparing the construction site—clearing the area of tall grass and removing several of the smaller trees.

Walking closer, I saw the excavation for the large foundation tier. It was huge! Peering over the side, I was relieved to see the dirt was firm and stable. Surprisingly, the hole was relatively free of debris, and the dimensions looked to be correct—seemingly ready for the stones and cement. Then, walking cautiously over to the bank of the river, I noticed the area had been rid of the large black ants which were crawling everywhere last April. I still remembered the one ant biting into my finger while I was trying to steady the Abney Level on the small, homemade survey rod. That bite actually brought a small amount of blood to the surface.

Looking at the river, I could easily tell this was the dry season, since the river was merely a small stream. Stepping across on the stone path, we made our way to the other side. To my amazement, the communities had fully excavated this foundation tier as well, somehow chiseling their way through a meter of shale rock. All at once, a really big smile came on my face, realizing how unimaginably difficult digging this foundation, using only picks and shovels, must have been. Several large piles of rock around the excavation revealed something about these people . . . their desire to see this bridge built.

As we left the bridge site that day, I stared back at the excavation area and the large piles of stones and thought to myself, *Raising the $25,000 . . . that now seemed to be the easy part of the project.* If it was hard for me to grasp how we were going to build this bridge by hand, then I couldn't imagine how the men and women digging the foundations and gathering the stones must feel. Did they really understand the enormity of this project and the amount of manual labor that will be required to complete it? And if the daily progress slowed any, will they continue to be committed or would they get discouraged and want to quit? For the communities of Gavilan and Patastule, building the bridge was going to be a daunting task. At this point, even I was starting to feel a little bit overwhelmed. Knowing that Milosz with Bridges to Prosperity would be here on Monday to help organize and get the construction started was a soothing thought.

The e-mail I received the next day from Milosz would quickly unnerve me. In his e-mail he stated that he was in the middle of two projects in El Salvador and starting a third, and wouldn't be in Matiguas until Friday. Then he asked for a favor . . . for me to start the construction of one foundation tier. I took a really deep breath as I continued reading his instructions.

The first part of his instructions was easy—simply to verify the dimensions of the excavation—5.1 meters by 3.6 meters by 1.0 meter deep—and check that it was square. Then came the more challenging parts—arrange with the municipality the services of a stonemason, buy as much cement and sand as I had money to purchase, and have both delivered to the bridge site. Then the more detailed part—begin the tier construction by building up the meter tall masonry walls, sixty centimeters wide.

Milosz gave me a vote of confidence by reminding me of the training I got in El Charcon, and that I should have gained enough experience there to handle this. Though I *had* spent twelve days before Thanksgiving working on the El Charcon Suspended Bridge in El Salvador, at this moment I wished I had taken more notes.

The first order of business that Monday morning was to visit the *Alcaldía* of Matiguas. We needed to hire a stonemason for the construction and hoped they would know of a good one. The stonemason was the key to the project's success, as he would essentially be the project's superintendent, each day directing and supervising the volunteer labor from the Gavilan and Patastule communities. In return for his skills and management role, Bridges to Prosperity would pay him a fair hourly wage from the bridge fund. For this reason, it was important to hire a stonemason with good leadership skills and who would work as hard, if not harder, than everyone else. More importantly, a person who could keep the community motivated.

For almost thirty minutes, Mike and Danilo discussed the bridge project's details with the town officials. Soon, a clean cut, well shaven man appeared in the doorway. He was introduced, and from what I could gather from the conversation, a stonemason. But for some reason, based purely on my first impression, I couldn't picture him being the right person for the job. Nevertheless, this is who the *Alcaldía* was recommending, and at this point, we didn't have any reason to question their recommendation.

With that order of business behind us, one of the officials took out a book. As he opened it and began to flip through its pages, I realized it contained pictures of rivers. He continued flipping through the pages until he stopped at one in particular. The picture before me was of an existing bridge crossing over a river gorge. Mike listened carefully as the official explained the relevance of the photo.

After a few minutes, Mike turned to me and explained that the bridge in the photo is in need of repair, and he would like for us to build a new bridge at this location after we complete the bridge for the Gavilan and Patastule communities. Without even taking a second to think, I looked at Mike and stated, "No! These people have a bridge. We are going to help build bridges for communities who don't have a bridge. And the location I choose to build the next bridge is going to be based on need . . . on the number of people it will help, and NOT based on who lives there." After Mike got through telling him my response, the man closed the book.

As we were leaving, I reminded Mike to ask them about buying a truck load of sand and where to buy the bags of cement. Their providing us with this information would make our meeting at least seem somewhat productive to me, as I still had concerns about the stonemason they had recommended. As he stood in the doorway, he struck me as too clean cut. I didn't need a bridge supervisor; I needed a person who was willing to get in the trench and show these two communities how to lay stones and build this bridge.

CHAPTER NINETEEN

PREPARING FOR CONSTRUCTION

The hardware store was only a short drive from the *Alcaldía*'s office. Inside the store reminded me of the hardware stores in Blythewood, only on a much smaller scale. One obvious difference was the absence of shelves; almost everything was displayed on the walls. I assume this was so the workers could watch people as they entered and easily tell what they were picking up to potentially purchase.

The right wall was covered with a large assortment of small hand tools, while the left wall was covered with all kinds of plumbing supplies. Seeing Mike and Danilo negotiating with the storeowner over the price for the bags of cement, I took my time looking over both walls to see if I saw anything I thought might be needed at the bridge site.

Before the trip, I had purchased several tools at the hardware store in Blythewood, including a hammer and masonry trowel—to replace the ones I left at the bridge site in El Salvador. I had also purchased an inexpensive carpenter's framing square, because I remembered in El Salvador trying to square the end of the walking planks with a metal ruler, and thinking at that moment I would have given $20 for a framing square.

After scanning over the tool wall several times, I saw two critical items—a package containing a roll of string and a line level. The string and line level would be needed in laying out the walls of the foundation tier. These two items, though simple, would be invaluable during this stage of the construction.

As I walked up to the counter with the package, Mike held out his hand, gesturing me for money. The total for the twenty bags of cement was almost two-hundred dollars, which was almost as much as I had left for the week. Since I had already paid in advance for the motel, I handed him the remaining one hundred-dollar bills from my wallet. This was another step of faith—that Milosz would arrive on Friday to repay me from the bridge account.

With the materials for the project now purchased, Mike and Danilo drove me back to the bridge site. Once there, Mike informed me of his travel plans for the week. He had explained to me earlier that Danilo wanted to show him other work projects in Managua, possibly for future mission teams. We then talked about my work schedule, the places I would eat, and my transportation to the bridge site each day. I could tell he was really making sure that he felt comfortable leaving me alone in the foreign town of Matiguas for four days. Personally—knowing I was called by God to be here and help these people build a bridge—I was not afraid of anything.

As the van was leaving, I let out a sigh of relief. I needed some time alone at the river to not only thank God for this opportunity, but to observe a moment of silence to remember all the ones who had drowned over the decades trying to cross the river. Maybe, too, for a mental reality check of being a complete stranger to these communities—coming from a world away—to show them how to build a pedestrian walking bridge.

It wasn't long before a gentleman came down, greeting me with a firm handshake. He was an elder from the Gavilan community, the one on the far-side of the river. As I smiled and looked into his eyes, I imagined the stories he could tell me of his people struggling to cross the river in the winter months—if only I knew more Spanish.

Standing there together, I pointed to the river and said a name as if asking a question, "Orlando?" There was an eerie moment of silence before he softly replied, "*Sí*," pointing down the river. There was nothing more to say, even if I could have.

Turning around, I heard the sound of a truck. It was "big" Oscar. I gave him this nickname because the driver of Danilo's passenger van is also named Oscar, though he is not nearly as round. As the truck rolled to a stop, I quickly peered in the back. Twenty bags of cement, forty-two and one-half kilograms (approximately ninety-four pounds) per bag. With the help of four other men, it took less than ten minutes to unload the truck.

Needing a break, I took the opportunity to take a picture of Santos standing beside the stacks of cement. He put on a big smile for the camera. I gently smiled back at him, knowing it would take more than ten times this amount to finish the bridge.

Not knowing when the sand or the stonemason would arrive, I signaled for everyone to follow me down to the near-side excavation. A massive pile of stones was in front of the excavation pit, wrapping partially around one side. Most of the larger stones had already been placed close to the excavation pit, so I first motioned for these to be pushed over the edge. These larger stones would be used to form the sixty-centimeter (twenty-four inches) thick walls of the foundation tier.

Then I demonstrated how the other stones needed to be sorted into smaller piles—one pile for the small stones and one pile for the medium stones. I reasoned that, by sorting the stones in this way, it would be easier for the community to recognize which size they needed to gather more of each day, though I had already observed a need to gather more of the larger stones.

Let me take this moment to say that gathering stones is probably the most grueling and back-breaking work in building one of these suspended bridges. I remembered at the El Charcon bridge site in El Salvador, the team would gather the large stones out of the river for several hours each morning and several hours each afternoon. Having a weak back, I would motion for one of the younger men to get me a big stone. It became almost a game as each time I would signal "larger," and they would struggle to dig out a river stone they thought I couldn't carry. If they could get in on my shoulder, I would carry it.

We spent the rest of that Monday afternoon sorting through the stone pile, including discarding the bad ones, meaning the sand stones. Sand stones are easy to pick out due to their light yellow appearance and also the characteristic of breaking apart very easily when dropped or hit with a hammer. Once I pointed out these were not suitable to build with, a discard pile was started just for them.

Later that evening as I packed my backpack to leave, I reviewed the checklist from Milosz. The only thing I could actually check off at this point was the cement, since it was now at the bridge site. Hopefully the sand and stonemason would show up tomorrow so the construction of the near-side foundation could begin. Anticipating that happening, I quickly checked the dimensions of the excavation. The dimensions were close, though one side appeared to need a little more dirt removed to make the wall straight. Since it was already late in the evening, this was something that could be verified in the morning.

Climbing back out of the excavation, I saw Santos waving for me to come to the road. He was standing beside a young man on a dirt bike. The young man was his son, and this would be my mode of transportation to and from the bridge site each day. I honestly couldn't remember the last time I had ridden on the back of a motorcycle, yet alone a dirt bike. Quickly adjusting my backpack and other belongings, we slowly started off. The four-mile ride back to town was bumpy, but the sun setting behind the Nicaraguan mountains made it not only tolerable, but enjoyable.

CHAPTER TWENTY

THE SAND ARRIVES

I awoke Tuesday morning to the sounds of a crowing rooster and a bus honking its horn for riders—the sounds of a new day in this developing country, with the sun ready to rise and give light to some kind of new hope. Getting the bridge construction started today would at least give two communities in Nicaragua a renewed sense of hope—that they'd not been forgotten amongst all the hustle and bustle in life, often referred to as "the American dream."

The motorcycle ride to the bridge site that morning allowed me the opportunity to fully enjoy the beauty of the mountain chain which surrounded the town of Matiguas. The morning sun provided a spectacular sight as it began to peek over these mountains. I tapped Santos' son on the shoulder almost a dozen times along the way, signaling him to stop and allow me to take photographs. After taking several, I quickly realized that no photo could ever fully capture the magnificent beauty of the sun's beams as they radiated through the low hanging clouds that surrounded the mountain tops.

Arriving at the bridge site, I saw Santos waiting for me, ready to get started. Though I had no idea when the sand or stonemason would arrive, I decided to start marking off the walls for the foundation tier. Santos held one end of the tape measure while I read the other as we checked the length of each side of the excavation against the drawing. Satisfied with these measurements, we verified the depth of the excavation in several places, which averaged one meter.

In Milsoz's instructions, the walls for the foundation tier needed to be sixty centimeters in width. I measured the sixty centimeters from the sides of the excavation, and Santos marked the measurement by drawing a line in the dirt with a stick. Once we finished, the lines formed a near perfect rectangle within the earthen walls of the excavation. A small stone was placed on the ground to mark each of the inside corners of this rectangle. At this point, I chuckled because I now needed four small pieces of lumber to drive in the ground at these corners, something sturdy to tie the string around.

Then I realized what we were building—a stone foundation wall—not a brick wall for a house. I also remembered where we were building it. With these two thoughts in mind, I signaled for Santos to cut me four long sticks from the tree branches lying on the ground nearby. Within minutes, Santos was holding four relatively straight sticks of equal length, with a point whittled on one end to make hammering them into the ground a little easier. It still amazed me to see how these people used a machete like I would a handsaw or chainsaw.

By this time, a lot of people from both communities had arrived to help. I noted the previous day a few tree limbs and a group of smaller trees which might interfere with the bridge's walking platform, so I went and showed several of the men what needed to be cut—using their machetes of course. The others continued sorting through the stone pile, which was still quite large. Everyone was willing to help, which was quite encouraging to me.

In the short amount of time it took me to give instructions to the others, Santos had driven two of the sticks at the locations we had marked with the small stones. Climbing back down into the excavation, I helped him drive the remaining two sticks using the same stone he had used for a hammer. Then I pulled the package with the string and line level from my backpack.

I securely tied the end of the string to one stick at the approximate height of one of the larger stones and pulled the string across to the adjacent stick. Santos held the string tight while I placed the line level on the string. I signaled for Santos to slowly raise the string he was holding, until the bubble was exactly in the middle of the two lines on the level. Santos wrapped the string around the second stick several times, and then pulled it across the length of the foundation to the third stick. We repeated the leveling process and then cut and tied the string back to the first stick. After re-checking the string on each side with the line level, I exited the excavation and took a few pictures. I have to admit, the sticks and string marking off the foundation walls was something I would only expect to see at a construction site in a developing country.

With the walls of the bridge's foundation tier now marked off, we carried and tossed more of the larger stones into the excavation. Having a reservoir of the larger stones would hopefully make building the walls a little faster, whenever that would be. We carried stones for almost an hour while others continued sorting the stone pile. Suddenly, everyone stopped what they were doing and listened, looking towards the road. It was a large covered truck carrying . . . the SAND!

Thankfully, Santos took charge, showing the driver the area already cleared of debris near a large tree. The location for the sand pile was a good distance from the main construction area, meaning it would not be in the way of other material deliveries. I watched as the driver slowly backed down the hill towards the tree. After the truck stopped, I was quick to notice that it wasn't equipped with a dump bed. However, I was relieved when two men appeared from the truck and jumped in the back with their shovels. As they began shoveling I remember thinking, *This could take them all day.*

Meanwhile, other volunteers stayed busy gathering more stones. The bridge design on this side of the river called for four tiers with a long approach ramp, meaning a lot of stones were needed. The approach ramp also required that a large area be cleared from behind the tiers, which included a farmer's barbed wire fence. The farmer had graciously donated the land for the bridge and had also agreed to have the fence relocated. A few of the men were already cutting and driving new posts in preparation for relocating the fence.

After several hours of moving stones, I went back to the delivery truck to check the progress of unloading the sand. To my surprise, the back of the truck was nearly empty, with one man beginning to sweep out the remnant from the front of the truck bed. I began inspecting the granularity of the black sand when the truck driver came over to me and started speaking to me in English. I was startled before asking him how he learned his English. He said he had spent several years working in the United States as a truck driver and had returned and married a woman from Nicaragua. He chose to live in Matiguas because he liked the lifestyle of the people there.

Then, of course, he wanted to know why I was here and what was being built. I spent the next ten minutes explaining my involvement in the footbridge project and how it would be built by the people in the communities. He was amazed that a church from the United States would not only raise the money, but actually come up into the mountains of Nicaragua and help the communities build the bridge. Then I explained my church's decade-long history of doing mission work in Nicaragua and some of the other completed projects.

As I continued to run my hands through the coarse sand, I remembered using a screen-sifter at the bridge site in El Salvador. The screen-sifter, with wood sides and a full screen bottom, was used to sift out the larger grains of sand, allowing the finer granules to pass through. The finer sand would be mixed with the bags of the cement, making the mortar to be used in the construction of the bridge's stone foundation walls.

Getting the stone foundation walls started this week now not only depended on hiring a stonemason who would actually show up for work, but getting a screen-sifter made. This being the case, I asked the truck driver if he would give me a ride back to town. He obliged and insisted I ride in the truck's cab rather than in the back with the other workers.

On the windshield of his truck was a large decaled sticker of Jesus wearing a crown of thorns. I was intrigued that someone would put this depiction on their vehicle's windshield, so I pointed to it. He looked over at me and asked, "Jesus . . . the same as your Jesus?" I replied, "Yes, the same. The Son of God—died on the cross—on the third day, rose from the grave, and is now in Heaven." He simply smiled and nodded his head.

Then I showed him the picture I had taken with my phone of the small hardware store where the cement had been purchased. Thankfully he knew exactly where it was located. I had already learned that when you're in a foreign country knowing less than twenty real words of their language or have no idea where anything is located, a picture IS worth a thousand words.

CHAPTER TWENTY-ONE

THE SCREEN-SIFTER

In town, the streets were busy with delivery trucks, but the driver managed to pull the truck right in front of the hardware store. I thanked him, even offering a few dollars for the ride—but he refused, saying he was glad that he could help me. As an American, I had already come to realize that the townspeople are generally willing to help you find what you need, especially when they know you are here to help their people.

As I exited the truck, I almost forgot the black plastic bag filled with sand. One of the men whistled and handed it to me from the back of the truck, where he had kept it from spilling. This sample of sand would be used to ensure I got the correct screen size for the screen-sifter. Basically, if the holes in the screen were too small, then none of the sand would go through—and if too big, then too many of the large pebbles would pass.

Before going into the hardware store, I found a clear area beside the sidewalk to place my backpack, my plastic lunch bag, and the bag of sand. Then I armed myself with my notebook, pen, and Spanish-English dictionary. Walking on nothing but faith and knowing I'm called to build this bridge, I walked toward the entrance to the hardware store. As I went to walk inside, I became elated. Sitting directly to the right of the entrance was a rack displaying four different size rolls of screened wire. This was going to be much easier than I had imagined.

The storeowner saw me and came to see what I needed. I placed my hand on the medium size screen, indicating for him to cut only a small piece. I went and got the bag of sand, hoping he would understand; thankfully, he did. I took the small piece of screen and the sand and knelt down beside the sidewalk. I slowly poured a handful of sand onto the screen, watching the smaller granules flow easily through while the larger pebbles remained on top. Perfect.

Satisfied this was the correct size, I told the storeowner, "Three feet." Realizing he obviously didn't understand, I re-stated the amount in Spanish, "*Uno metro.*" Within seconds, I was holding one meter of the screen. Then I remembered at the construction site in El Salvador, the screen-sifter was badly worn from extended use, the screen having several rips and a large tear. With this in mind, I told him, "*Dos*," or "Two." Having two screen-sifters at the bridge site would not only speed up the process of sifting the sand, but provide a spare if one became damaged.

Now all I needed was a couple of two-by-fours to make the wooden frames. Taking out my notebook, I sketched a square frame and said, "Wood." He just stared at me. I quickly looked up "wood" in the English part of the dictionary, and tried to pronounce the Spanish word "*madera*." He looked puzzled, so I showed him the word in my dictionary. Now he better understood my sketch and pointed down the street. As I looked down the street, I didn't see anything that looked like a lumber yard. I turned back to him and gestured "where?" He smiled and pointed at the next cross street and started counting and hand-signaling, "*Uno . . . dos . . . tres*." I smiled and repeated his instructions to show I understood. Now realizing the lumber yard was on the third street over, I paid him for the two pieces of screen and began walking in that direction.

After walking past the third street, I could see where the street seemingly turned to dirt. Thinking maybe I was supposed to turn down the third street, I went back. As I turned to walk down that street, I heard someone say, "Hey man." I quickly turned around to see three young girls sitting inside their family's small convenience store. They were all giggling because one of them had just said something in English to me, and I had actually turned around to acknowledge the statement.

Looking over at them, I could quickly tell they had begun to feel uncomfortable, so I approached the open-fronted store slowly. For a moment we just looked at one another, none knowing what to say next. Then one of the girls excitedly pointed to the plastic bag I was toting. I knew exactly what she was looking at . . . my leftover bread rolls from breakfast. I handed her the bag, then pulled out my Spanish-English dictionary—now I needed her help. After explaining the best I could "lumber" and trying to better pronounce the word "*madera*," she pointed down the street towards where the pavement ended. I thanked her and once again started walking.

Just before the pavement ended there was a woodworking shop. The workers were busy planing rough-cut lumber, making each side smooth and even. This appeared to be a "professional" wood working shop, at least the best I was going to find in this town. I watched in the doorway for several minutes before a worker finally noticed me, prompting him to get the shop's owner.

The saws made it very noisy and difficult for us to greet one another, so the owner and I stepped outside. The noise from the saws really didn't bother me since I only knew a handful of words in Spanish. Once outside, I showed him the two pieces of screen, the bag of sand, and a sketch of what I needed him to build. He studied the sketch of what I saw as a screen-sifter. At that moment, I remembered the screen-sifter in El Salvador lacked an easy way to hold it while moving it back and forth, so I tried to indicate the need for handles by drawing lines on each end. I also remembered the screen was not attached to the wooden frame very well, so I wanted this one to be more rugged and reinforced—the screen securely attached to the frame.

As we both struggled to understand one another, a young man suddenly appeared who knew perfect English and Spanish. After about five minutes of him translating, the woodshop's owner redrew the frame, his showing detailed handles and explaining that it would be well built. Now the only question I had was, "How much for two?" Speaking through the translator, he said he would make two for 500 *córdobas*, or about $23. That seemed like a lot to me, so I told him it was for the bridge at the Bulbul River. The young man interpreted my negotiating statement, and the owner agreed to make them for 400 *córdobas*, about $9 each, since it was for the bridge. We shook hands and I thanked him. As I gathered my backpack to leave, I asked when I could pick them up. No interpreter was needed for his response, "*Tres*," or "Three."

After finishing our conversation, I stood there for a moment . . . amazed at what had just taken place. Starting the construction on the bridge this week depended on getting the screen-sifters made. Now not only were they getting made, but I would be able to pick them up in less than three hours. Then I realized I needed something other than a motorcycle to carry them to the bridge site . . . I needed a truck. Once again, I was depending on God to put the people in my path who could help me.

Walking and looking in the direction of the town square, I saw the church steeple in the distance. For some reason I didn't feel comfortable walking alone on this street, so I stopped for a moment to consider my options and say a short prayer. Lifting my head up, I couldn't believe my eyes . . . it was Danilo's van. At that moment I'm really not sure whose eyes were bigger, but I believe Oscar's were . . . not believing I was walking alone in this part of town.

I did the best I could to explain to him why I was here, pointing to the woodshop and then showing him the sketch of the screen-sifter. I could tell he had no idea what he was looking at, but only hoped he understood that I needed to be back here at three o'clock to pick up the pieces and take them to the bridge site. Of course it really didn't matter, because the stonemason had once again not shown up for work. Though I knew how to hand mix the concrete and place the stones, I was only here for a week. This project needed an experienced stonemason who could organize the daily work activities and supervise the volunteers from the communities.

It was past time for lunch, so I had Oscar drop me off at the café. As I was sitting and enjoying a sandwich, a Nicaraguan businessman walked in from the street and sat down at my table. He had seen me in town and wanted to know what I was working on, and if I needed any help. We talked for probably thirty minutes on everything from politics to poverty. I showed him pictures of the bridge construction and explained my church's involvement. He was amazed, and as he was leaving, he thanked me for coming and helping his people.

Finishing the last bite of my sandwich, I took out my phone and checked the time and for any new messages. I still had over an hour before needing to be back at the woodshop. At that moment, Danilo's wife stepped outside to greet me and ask how things were going at the bridge. I told her I needed to speak to Mike. Before I could say another word, she was pushing the numbers on her cell phone and handing me the phone.

Danilo answered, "*Hola.*" Hearing my voice he immediately handed the phone to Mike. I explained to Mike that the stonemason had not shown up for work either day, but most of the preparation work had been completed—checking the dimensions of the excavation, laying out the walls of the foundation tier, and sorting the stone pile. Now I needed for Danilo's truck to meet me at the woodshop at three o'clock to pick up the screen-sifters and take them to the bridge site. Our conversation ended with me explaining to him the location of the woodshop, and him assuring me the truck would be there at three o'clock.

During our conversation, Mike couldn't believe the stonemason had not shown up for work, but was pleased at how much I had gotten done and told me I was doing a good job. Those words were all I needed to hear . . . to know Mike was pleased with the progress of the construction.

As I walked back to the woodshop that afternoon, I kept reminding myself that the bridge wasn't going to be built in a month, or even two months. My assignments from Milosz were to get the construction site organized, purchase the sand and cement, and hire a stonemason who would supervise the workers from the community. If I could accomplish all of this, then I would be leaving on Friday with a big smile on my face.

CHAPTER TWENTY-TWO

CONSTRUCTION BEGINS

Wednesday morning I again awoke to the sounds of roosters crowing and a bus honking its horn for riders. But the knocking at my door early in the night, though at first frightening me, brought the best news of all. Standing at my door was a member of the *Alcaldía* and a man he introduced as my new stonemason, Carlos. Carlos was wearing an old T-shirt and appeared slightly overweight, but this time, I immediately knew in my heart he was the right man sent for the job. After a firm handshake, he agreed to meet me at seven o'clock to have breakfast at the café.

During breakfast, I showed Carlos several pictures on my phone taken of the bridge construction in El Charcon, El Salvador, including pictures of the stones used to build the main structures. He was amazed at the large stone tiers and the tall stone walls of the approach ramp. I pointed at the picture on my phone and then at him, as if to ask, "Can you build this?" "*Sí*," was his response, showing a slight grin.

The ride to the bridge site that morning was again a time for me to enjoy looking at the beautiful mountains and the rising sun, a chance to take in the splendor of God's creation. I felt so blessed to be given this opportunity, to be able to give back to God's people a portion of the blessings I had received in my own life.

Arriving at the bridge site, I saw that Santos had already arranged the wheel barrow, shovels, and one screen-sifter. Others had completed nailing a large portion of the barbed wire fence to the new posts. With most of the site preparation work now completed and a new stonemason hired, we were finally ready to begin the construction.

Carlos arrived not long after I did. We walked down to the bridge site where I showed him the excavation, the stone piles, and the sand. I introduced him to Santos and then to the other workers. At that moment I looked over at Santos and told him, "*Dos cemento.*" Santos turned and instructed one of the men. Within minutes, the man had returned with the wheel barrow loaded with two bags of cement.

Walking over to the sand pile, I pointed at the small cleared area and said, "*Plástico*." Santos acknowledged, "*Sí*." This time, Santos went himself up the hill to the small block house where the construction tools and other materials were stored. He returned with a large piece of black plastic, placing it on the ground in front of the pile of sand.

I picked up the screen-sifter and motioned for Santos to grab the other end. Carlos instinctively grabbed the shovel and scooped a shovel of sand into the screen-sifter. After a few failed attempts, Santos learned the shaking motion required to move the larger pebbles in the screen-sifter around so that the smaller granules of sand could freely fall through the screen. The large pebbles were then discarded by simply flipping the screen-sifter over.

The sifted sand formed a pile on the black plastic, where it could be easily shoveled into the five-gallon buckets without any dirt or grass contaminants. The whole process would be repeated until eight buckets were filled and emptied in a pile nearer the excavation. The eight buckets equaled the amount of sand needed to make one batch of mortar, which is commonly referred to as *mezcla*, or mixture. The sand to cement ratio in one batch of mortar is four-to-one, thus the need to buy the whole truckload of sand.

Everyone took turns shoveling sand into the screen-sifter, using the screen-sifter, and carrying the buckets filled with sand to the cleared area beside the excavation. When the eighth bucket of sand was emptied onto the pile, the two bags of cement were busted open and poured onto the pile. The sand and cement were then slowly mixed together like the sugar and flour of a homemade cake. As the light gray cement was folded in with the black sand, the mixture's color became a dark gray.

I knew Carlos had done this before because it would have been very difficult for me to explain the next step—making the infamous "volcano." Though none of the design manuals I had read recommended this method of mixing the cement, this appeared to be the method of choice in developing countries like El Salvador and Nicaragua. After thoroughly mixing the sand and cement, Carlos took his shovel and began pulling the powdery mix away from the center, forming the walls of the volcano. Then, he took a five-gallon bucket that had been filled with water from the river and poured it in the center. He did the same with the second bucket of water, this time pouring more slowly . . . careful not to stress the walls of the volcano.

Carlos let the water soak into the wall of sand for several minutes. This gave me a chance to reflect back to the construction at the El Charcon Bridge in El Salvador—counting in my mind how many "volcanoes" I helped mix. As Carlos began moving his shovel around the outer wall, I remembered thinking, *Now the real work begins.* I grabbed the shovel from Santos and began helping Carlos fold-in the outer edges, putting more and more of the dry sand-cement mixture into the watery center. It was a slow process—shovel too much or too quickly and the volcano's wall would break, causing a big "lava" flow.

Eventually, the wall was intentionally broken to allow for all of the dry mixture to be thoroughly mixed with the water. Once this was done, shoveling and folding the heavy mixture became much harder and tiresome. Thankfully, two men stepped forward to grab the shovels and help finish the mixing process. The only test for the mixture's consistency was dipping a masonry trowel into the mortar and judging how firm it appeared as it rolled off the edge of the trowel. If it was too dry—sprinkle in more water . . . too wet—add in more sand. After about ten minutes, the first official batch of mortar was ready.

Carlos was the first to jump into the excavation and start standing up the larger, flatter stones—placing one beside the other. To my surprise, it only took three of the large stones to make the width of the sixty-centimeter foundation wall. (Note: A stone is weakest when laid flat and strongest when stood on its side.) Having helped lay the stones in the approach walls for the bridge in El Salvador, I could tell Carlos knew exactly what he was doing.

After standing enough stones to form the first ten feet of the foundation wall, Carlos grabbed a bucket he had filled with mortar and began pouring it over the stones. The mortar was slightly soupier in consistency than what would be used in building a brick wall, but its purpose was not to make a thick mortar joint between the stones, but to serve as a bonding agent for the stones.

Making an observation, I stopped Carlos and grabbed a few of the smaller stones and showed him how they could be used to fill in the voids between the larger stones. Simply taking a little extra time to fill these voids would not only reduce the amount of mortar wasted running into these voids, but in the end, would save the project money. Carlos nodded his head in agreement and grabbed a handful of the smaller stones to show the other men, which now gave everyone something to do.

By the end of the day, one complete layer of stone and mortar had been completed for the entire circumference of the foundation tier. With the start of the second layer of stones, the walls were now well-defined. Most notable of the day's progress was that the center of the excavation was almost completely vacant of the larger stones.

Packing my tools, I saw Carlos checking the dimensions of the foundation. He suddenly appeared to be upset. I hurriedly jumped into the excavation to try and understand the problem. With his tape measure, he hastily measured the length of the wall's interior—the two longer interior sides were not the same length. I helped him measure across each diagonal, to make sure the foundation was square . . . it wasn't. Somehow I had made an error when laying out the foundation tier. Since it was time to go home, I simply stated, "*Mañana*," or "Tomorrow."

That night in my motel room, I re-opened the e-mail on my phone from Milosz, which showed all of the dimensions of the bridge's foundation tier. I carefully made a sketch in my notebook, calculating the measurements for the interior diagonals and labeling all the lengths in centimeters. Based on my field notes taken the previous day, the overall excavation measured slightly larger than it needed to be, which was good.

For the foundation tier in the ground, I knew the outer dimensions weren't as significant as the inner ones. One crucial detail was that the rectangle formed by the inner walls of the foundation tier needed to be perfectly square, since the second tier's walls would be inset half of the width of the foundation tier's walls, which for this reason were required to be a minimum of sixty centimeters wide. In order for the mechanical forces of the bridge's cables and walking platform to be evenly distributed throughout the tiered structure, each tier had to be constructed on top of the previous tier in this manner. The finished tiered structure would actually resemble a traditional wedding cake. So with each tier affecting the next, any discrepancies between the design and what was already built had to be resolved.

I arrived early to the bridge site Thursday morning, hoping to be there before Carlos—but I wasn't. Carlos had already helped Santos bring all of the construction tools down from the small house near the bridge site—which had an attached room with a door that could be locked. Carlos and Santos were now busy sifting more sand to be mixed with the four bags of cement stacked nearby. I showed them a big smile and a thumbs-up as I walked over to the excavation pit, hoping only minor corrections would be needed. Three young men were there tossing more of the larger stones into the middle of the excavation. I simply said, "*Alto*," which means "Stop," before climbing into the excavation. Carlos was right behind me.

I pulled out my notebook and showed Carlos the sketch of the foundation, pointing to the measurements labeled on each side, including on the diagonals. We first measured the overall length and width of the excavation itself. I already knew these were good but needed for Carlos to put his trust in the dimensions I had labeled on the sketch.

I recorded all the measurements and then wrote each one beside the corresponding location on the sketch. I showed Carlos that each of our measurements were slightly greater than those on the sketch, and then gave him the thumbs-up sign. I already knew the width of the walls were ten centimeters more than required by the design, which would compensate for the larger-than-needed excavation. The interior measurements were next.

We measured the interior wall of the one side I knew was correct. To my surprise, three of the interior wall's lengths were correct, which relieved Carlos of his initial concerns (*as well as my own*). This meant none of our work from the previous day would have to be re-done. The fourth side's interior measurement, however, was fifteen centimeters (about six inches) too long. I recorded these measurements directly on the sketch.

As I studied the sketch, it immediately became apparent to me what needed to be done to correct the foundation. To make the interior rectangle truly square and the tier dimensions correct for the placement of the next tier, all we needed was to construct one additional row of stones on the inside of the back wall. Santos helped me measure and move one corner stick the needed fifteen centimeters; this was all that was needed to square-up the foundation tier.

Since I felt fully responsible for the confusion this mistake had caused, I took it upon myself to fix it. I picked a couple of skinny stones that were tall and close to the needed width and stood them on their end. I got a bucket, filled it with freshly mixed mortar, and quickly added some mortar to the first layer.

As I looked at the progress I had made and how good a job I was doing, I decided to go ahead and add a second layer of stones, just to bring my work even with Carlos' progress for that morning. However, as I quickly found out, it is very important to let the mortar sufficiently dry before adding additional layers of stones. As I placed the last stone to complete the second layer of the small addition, the stones in the first layer started to shift. I quickly sat down and pressed my chest against the wall of stones, stretched out both arms and placed my hands on two of the larger stones.

I did everything possible to prevent the stones from falling, but it was too unstable. The stones and wet mortar came crumbling down, landing either in my lap or around where I was sitting; the addition to the interior wall was now a complete mess. Carlos came over and grinned, then handed me another bucket of mortar so that I could start over. Within ten minutes, I had once again completed the first layer of stones, but this time, I stopped and let the mortar dry for several hours before adding the second layer.

By the end of the work day on Thursday, the string had once again been raised, and work had started in one corner on the fourth layer of stones. I took a few pictures of the foundation with my phone before packing up my tools. Walking to the road to wait for my ride back to town I felt kind of sad, knowing this was my last work day at the bridge. But looking back at the construction site, I became excited—anxious to e-mail Milosz the pictures showing our progress.

That night in bed, I reflected back on everything that had happened in the past year surrounding the bridge project: the site survey, the fundraising, and now the construction. The bridge project had not only given me fulfillment, but my heart was filled with joy. My pastor had already told me that the story of the ten one-dollar bills was an incredible story, but what about the rest of the story? Would anyone believe everything that had happened in my life surrounding the bridge project? Maybe my next calling would be to write that book I had told Avery someone needed to write during our trip last April—if the funds were raised and the bridge actually got built.

As thoughts of writing a book flowed through my mind, suddenly there was a BAM! BAM! BAM! Someone was banging heavily on my door, almost like they were trying to break it down. I leaped out of bed to my feet, and then another BAM! BAM! BAM! on the door, this time followed by, "HEY MAN . . . IT'S DAVE! . . . LET ME IN; NO MAN, DAVE AIN'T HERE." I wasn't sure who they were or what they wanted, but they obviously had the wrong room. As I slipped on my pants and made my way to the door, there was another BAM! BAM! BAM! on the door, followed again by, "NO MAN! IT'S ME! IT'S DAVE! . . . NO MAN, DAVE AIN'T HERE." This time, the voice sounded familiar, so I opened the door, shouting, "MIKE, IS THAT YOU?" "It's me," said Mike, "You obviously didn't have the 70's record album." I replied, "You're crazy . . . and I was a small kid then." We both laughed.

Before I could ask Mike any questions about where he had been, he told me he hadn't had a hot shower in three days and wanted to know if the hot water was fixed. He was really happy when I told him the repairman had replaced the "widow-maker." The "widow-maker" was what Mike called the attachment on the shower head, which contained a 4500 Watt heating element that heated the cold water running through it and out of the shower head.

Mike had explained to me that the reason he gave the water heating device the nickname of "widow-maker" was "because people reach up and touch it, and nothing in Nicaragua is grounded. You keep your hands off of it. You'll go some places where the wire nuts, wrapped with a little bit of tape, are sticking out of them. There have been people reach up and touch those things (the wire nuts) while they are taking a shower, and with poor wiring, they get fried in the shower. They're standing there being doused by water and then they grab electricity."

Thankfully, the rest of the night was uneventful, with Friday morning coming too soon. After being in the town of Matiguas for almost a week, it was now time for us to leave. After breakfast, we travelled to the bridge site in the van so Mike and Danilo could see the progress made on the bridge. At the bridge site, Mike was pleased to see the organization of the construction activities: some sifting sand, some mixing mortar, and others laying stones.

Carlos was busy re-tying the strings for the fourth stone layer, because we would remove the string each night for fear of someone stealing it. This meant each morning, we had the tedious task of tying the string back to the sticks, which gave everyone more practice using the line level. In fact, I had bought a new line level from the hardware store to replace the first, whose ends had come unglued from its plastic cylinder.

Using the new line level, I noticed as I was tying the string to the third stick that the string was slightly below the mark on the stick from the previous day. I knew something was definitely wrong when I leveled and tied the string back to the first stick that it was about four inches below where the starting string was tied. I placed the line level on the string between the first two sticks and then checked the remaining sides—all were exactly level. But if all of the strings were level, then why was the string from the fourth stick not landing at the starting string's position on the first stick? This didn't make any sense, so I reluctantly asked for Mike's help.

I explained to Mike my method of leveling the stone layers and then showed him the result after checking the last side. I told Mike we had done this every morning, and the only difference this morning was we were using a new line level. Mike asked to hold the small level, which had yellow colored ends. I went and got the broken level from my backpack, which had red ends and had come packaged with the string. I stuck the ends back on and once again checked the string—NOT level. Now, I was really puzzled. Two identical line levels, each bought from the same hardware store, but one indicating a different point of level than the other. How could I figure out which one was correct?

As I was thinking through possible solutions, I noticed Carlos and Charlie, also a stonemason, removing a clear, flexible hose from Carlos' bag of tools. The half-inch hose was probably twenty feet long but with no fitting on either end. Before I could ask Mike the question, he spoke up and said, "Now they are going to show you how they level things the Nicaraguan way." I gave a gentle grin, "With a hose?" Mike explained, "That's what they call a water-level. They are going to use the hose to check the position of the string at each corner of the foundation, and when they finish, the string will be more level than using your line level."

I watched as one of the workers took the hose down to the river and, using his mouth, slowly drew water into the hose, completely filling it with water. He placed a thumb over each end to prevent any water from escaping as he carried the hose up the hill from the river. At the excavation, he carefully handed each end of the hose to Carlos. Carlos held the ends upward as he removed his thumbs. Now, the water was free to move back and forth in the hose between the two ends. Carlos purposefully allowed a small amount of water to escape before handing one end to Charlie, who was waiting with me inside the foundation.

Carlos took the end he was holding and placed it up against the first stick. He showed me a black line marked just below the end of the hose and indicated for me to keep this line on the string's position for the fourth stone layer. Then, Carlos pointed for Charlie to place the other end on the second stick. As I watched the water inside the hose slowly moving above and then below the black line, I still didn't fully understand what we were doing.

As Charlie positioned his end of the hose against the second stick, Carlos looked for the water's position in my end. I pointed to where the water stopped in the hose, which was just below the black line. Carlos motioned for Charlie to start raising his end of the hose, and when the water reached the black line, he whistled for Charlie to stop. Carlos went and marked the second stick at the location of the water in the hose. This mark on the second stick was at the same height, or water level, as the water in my end and the string location on the first stick. Carlos moved the string up a little bit on the second stick to the new mark. Charlie then moved his end of the hose to the third stick, and then to the fourth. At each stick, Carlos marked the water level and raised the string to the new mark.

After Carlos had finished repositioning the string at each stick, I took the first line level, the one with the red ends, and placed it on the string between the first and second sticks. As the string settled, I watched as the bubble moving in the lime-green liquid inside of the plastic cylinder stopped exactly between the black lines, indicating the string was perfectly level. Then, I placed the second line level, the one Mike was holding with the yellow ends, on the same string. I was amazed as its bubble stopped beneath the black line, meaning it was wrong. I guess there's a first time for everything, right? But how could a level be wrong?

After Mike had finished inspecting the second level, he noticed its plastic cylinder wasn't perfectly round—it was, in fact, defective. What was even better was the fact that we proved the level was wrong by using a simple leveling technique using a clear hose the Nicaraguan people refer to as a water-level. And that line level, I gave it to one of the workers, who might trade it to an unsuspecting person for a candy bar.

As we were leaving the bridge site on the dirt road, we met up with Milosz from B2P. I introduced Milosz to Mike and we all shook hands. I explained to him the progress we had made since Monday, the materials we had purchased, and the name of our stonemason. Mike and I handed him the receipts from the purchases of the sand and cement, which he promptly reimbursed.

As we said our good-byes, Milosz thanked us both for our efforts in getting the project started. During this week, I had somehow accomplished everything I had wanted to accomplish. My work on this project was finished, and it was now up to these two communities to embrace this opportunity and build themselves a bridge.

CHAPTER TWENTY-THREE

GOD STILL MOVES MOUNTAINS

Getting back to the States, I didn't have much time to prepare for my church's monthly bridge update, which was scheduled for Sunday, February 20th. I decided the update would be the usual five minutes—which translated to one typed, single-spaced page. In it, I told of how hard the community had worked in digging the foundations for the bridge, and everything we had accomplished during my week at the bridge site. I emphasized that the community was taking full advantage of this opportunity to build themselves a bridge.

I then shared the expressed need for additional footbridges near the town of Matiguas. I introduced a unique fundraising concept I called "Vision 2012," with the tag line of "500 people giving $50. Will you be 'ONE'?" My idea was to challenge everyone to spread the need for these bridges to their family and friends, so more people could share in the blessings of helping their "neighbor" in a foreign land, simply enhancing the quality of these people's lives with a footbridge.

That night, after I had finished typing the bridge update, I called my dad and told him what had been accomplished during my trip. I could feel the excitement in his voice as I shared a lot of the construction details. As always, he told me how proud he was of me. Before hanging up, he asked if I would come and give an update at his church on a Wednesday night. I agreed, knowing that speaking at Jones Crossroads on a Wednesday night meant having to prepare a thirty-minute sermon.

I prayed that week for the message to share with his church. I last spoke there in May, when I preached *The Faith Message* and introduced the Nicaraguan bridge project, asking them to pray for the project and me. Since then, I hadn't shared with them any monthly updates or newsletter stories like I had for my church. However, I knew Dad had kept his pastor informed of the bridge's fundraising efforts. In fact, before leaving for

Nicaragua, I had personally called his pastor to tell him the story of the ten one-dollar bills, and how God had revealed his faithfulness through a simple car wash fundraiser.

The bridge fundraising had been a huge mountain in front of me and my church congregation. The biggest mountain I now saw was in not only getting the bridge construction started, but seeing if the community could actually build the bridge. Thinking of these two mountains, one Scripture came to mind: *"Jesus answered, 'Have faith in God. I tell you the truth, you can say to this mountain, "Go, fall into the sea." And if you have no doubts in your mind and believe that what you say will happen, God will do it for you. So I tell you to believe that you have received the things you ask for in prayer, and God will give them to you.'"* (Mark Chapter 11, Verses 20-24 NCV)

I titled the sermon, *God Still Moves Mountains.* The sermon included details from my own incredible faith journey over the past year: the search for purpose and direction, the vision God gave to me, the charge He presented me, and my prayer for Him to show me another mountain to climb. The mountain He showed to me was the bridge in Nicaragua, which included not only designing the bridge, but raising the money for the materials. In the sermon, I shared my own fears of stepping out of the boat, of what people would think, and the possible rewards for being a faithful servant. I told the story no one had ever heard—the story of the ten one-dollar bills.

I concluded the sermon by telling the congregation that all the money was raised and the bridge has now been started, followed by the statement, "Both of my mountains were not only moved, but God smoothed a road across what was left—God still moves mountains." With the sermon for Dad's church now finished, my thoughts turned to the message I would share with the Men's Ministry at Harmony Baptist Church on Sunday, February 27th.

Before leaving for Nicaragua, I had already written the February and March newsletter stories for my church. Since the March's newsletter story told the story of the ten one-dollar bills, I felt like I needed to share that story with my cousin, Bill. It was my and Bill's aunt who had given me the card with the money inside over twenty years ago. So the week before leaving for Nicaragua, I went to his house in Richburg to personally share the story with him and his family. I took a copy of the newsletter story that I could leave at their house in case they weren't home. After sitting in their driveway for a few minutes, I went and placed the folder containing the newsletter story on a chair beside the back door.

Several days went by without hearing from Bill. Then, the night before leaving for Nicaragua, he called. He said he read the newsletter story several times, and each time he cried, not truly believing what he was reading. He said it was an incredible story and was really glad that I had shared it with him. We talked for over thirty minutes, with me sharing about the mission project of building a pedestrian bridge in Nicaragua. So I was surprised when he called the next day asking me to come speak to his church's Men's Ministry. I agreed, and at that moment realized that the Lord had now provided two open doors to share with others not only about the mission project, but my faith experiences.

After preaching at Dad's church and speaking to the Men's Ministry at Harmony Baptist, several months passed. In Milosz's last e-mail, he stated that the communities were now gathering stones from all around the town of Matiguas due to lack of good stones at the Bulbul River. He also stated that the number of workers from the communities varied from day to day, and that these two problems had greatly slowed the bridge's construction; the project was now well behind schedule.

As the project coordinator responsible for getting this bridge built, I knew I needed to get back to Nicaragua and find out firsthand what all the problems were. I had enough vacation and money for one more trip to Nicaragua. I knew the rainy season would start during the month of May, and that getting the steel cables pulled across the river before then was crucial. After looking at my work calendar and the meetings I was responsible for attending, I decided on the second week in May. That night, I e-mailed Milosz with these dates so he could arrange for the cables to be delivered to the bridge site that week, and would be expecting me at the job site.

What I wasn't expecting was the phone call that week from my cousin, Bill. His first question was, "Tommy . . . is the bridge finished?" I knew by this question that he was genuinely interested in the bridge project and my mission work. "No Bill," I answered, "but I'm going to Nicaragua next week to help pull the cables across the river." He continued by saying he had been praying for me and my involvement with the bridge, and again appreciated me coming to speak at his church in February. He recommended a book that he thought I needed to read, *Build a Bridge and Get Over It!, written* by Dr. George H. Harris. He said the book was about building bridges, and since I was building a bridge, thought I might want to read it. I thanked him for recommending the book and told him I would buy it to read during my trip next week.

CHAPTER TWENTY-FOUR

GOING BACK TO FINISH THE BRIDGE

As I approached the ticket counter at the Charlotte-Douglas Airport, I could already feel my heartbeat starting to race. Though I had mentioned my travel plans of going to work on the bridge during the monthly bridge update, no one else had expressed any serious interest in going. For the first time, I was travelling alone to Nicaragua.

At the ticket counter, I checked in a suitcase and a large duffle bag. The suitcase contained all the clothes I would need for the work week, including an extra pair of shoes. The rolling duffle bag was packed absolutely full. In it were two cordless drill kits (drill, drill bits, battery charger, and two 18.0 Volt batteries), five fall-arrest lanyards, a masonry trowel, a hammer, cutting pliers, several hundred feet of pull-tape rope, a one hundred-meter tape measure, a hacksaw with an extra set of blades, a box containing a dozen new hats, and a variety of food staples. The food staples were actually each day's lunch, which included individual serving containers of applesauce, canned carrots, pudding cups, and tuna.

This now being my fourth trip out of the country in a little over a year, I knew exactly what I could and couldn't take on the airplane. For this reason, I had checked-in my entire luggage on the last two trips. This time, my duffle bag held everything I needed to finish the bridge, which meant for the first time I would have to carry my backpack onto the plane. The backpack was where I normally stored all of the tools needed for each trip (i.e. knife, pliers, hammer, tape measure, flashlight, extra batteries, and gloves). So that week at home, I had emptied everything out on the living room floor and re-packed the "safe" items, making sure I removed every tool, especially my pocket knife. In their place, I packed a hard plastic carpentry square, a scientific calculator, a handheld movie camera, and a clear plastic container packed with a variety of snacks for the trip.

As I patiently stood in the security checkpoint line, I went over in my mind everything I was bringing. The only thing I worried about passing through airport security was my duffle bag, since it contained the two drill kits, drill bits, rope, and hacksaw blades. All I could do was trust it would pass safely through security and be placed underneath the plane with the other luggage. Finishing the bridge depended on that bag getting to Nicaragua with all of its contents.

My real concern was being singled out at one of the security checkpoints, since I was travelling alone out of the country. Trying not to look nervous, I confidently placed my backpack onto the conveyor belt, took off my shoes, and stepped through the body scanner . . . no problem. Waiting for my backpack, I heard the security agent call the second agent over to look at the scanned image, pointing to the screen. Then the second security agent approached me and firmly asked, "Sir, what do you do and where are you going?" *There is obviously a problem with something packed in my backpack, but what?* I wondered.

With absolutely nothing to conceal, I answered, "I'm going to Nicaragua to work on a pedestrian walking bridge. I don't know what he sees on the screen, but all he should see are a flashlight, four AA batteries, gloves, tape measure, carpentry square, calculator, and some snacks." "That's not it," as the agent grabbed my backpack from the conveyor and proceeded to open it. As he started to inspect the contents, I leaned over to look with him. "Stand back, sir, STAND BACK!" instructed the first agent. At that moment, I realized this was serious; I could actually be detained. I felt helpless. I was completely at their mercy.

My concerns were alleviated as the security agent pulled the clear plastic container from my backpack, which I knew only contained snacks. But after removing the lid from the container, he reached in and pulled out a three inch long, cylindrically shaped metal object. Believe me—I was just as surprised to see that object as he was. As he continued holding the foreign object in front of me, I then realized exactly what it was. But at that moment I wasn't sure if any explanation would be sufficient for him, since it now appeared that I was trying to sneak the small object onto the plane in my snack container.

With nothing to lose but my freedom, I proceeded to explain the object, and hoped he would believe me and know my intentions were completely innocent. I simply stated, "That's a center punch." I paused briefly, trying to judge his demeanor. Seeing he appeared not to disagree,

I continued with a brief explanation of the intended use—"I have to drill holes in the wooden crossbeams for the bridge's walking planks, and the punch will be hit with a hammer at the center of the marked hole location, ensuring the drill bit doesn't drift after the drill is started."

At that moment I was scared to even breathe. He wasn't smiling. I was relieved when he finally spoke, "Yes . . . I know what this is, and I believe your explanation." *Whew!* After helping put everything back into my backpack, he smiled and wished me luck on the bridge. I thanked him and then hurried off to my flight's gate.

After checking in at the flight gate and taking a seat on the plane, I tried to remember the security checkpoints I would have to pass through at the other airports, including going through Customs and paying Nicaragua's fee to enter their country. Filling out the Customs form now almost seemed routine, as did the health advisory form which had checkboxes for having the common cold all the way down to being exposed to swine flu. I did realize one advantage I had over any previous trip: my passport now had a Customs stamp from Nicaragua and El Salvador, both obtained within the past year. This was hopefully an indication to the Customs agent that I wasn't simply a tourist going on vacation, but a business traveler who knew where he was going once he got inside the county.

No sooner had I boarded the plane in Charlotte than we were landing in Miami. Miami's airport was always heavily crowded, but I knew my way around; most importantly, how to get to the food court. At the food court, Mike and I would always eat at the same restaurant, which serves the best boneless chicken breast, mashed potatoes, and steamed broccoli. It was always a good "welcome back home" meal, too, since all we would get with our chicken in Nicaragua was white rice, red beans, and a slice of goat cheese.

Thinking of my past trips to Nicaragua always made the two-hour flight to Managua seem much shorter. Once I exited the plane, it was really easy to tell where to go next—just run with the crowd. Thankfully, the airport in Managua is small in comparison to the airports in Charlotte and Miami. But not only is it smaller, the airport's baggage check point method last year was archaic in comparison to those two modern airports.

On that trip to Nicaragua, there were two baggage check point lines, with several security officers manually checking each person's baggage. This seemed like a great idea until I ended up behind a family who had taken full advantage of protecting their luggage with the plastic protective wrapping service offered at the airport in Miami. I patiently waited as the security agents struggled to cut through all the layers of plastic sheeting just to get to the luggage. Thankfully, another security officer was paying attention and motioned for me to pass around them.

To my surprise, Managua's airport now had two automated baggage scanning machines at the security checkpoint, which appeared to speed things up for everyone. Placing my backpack on the conveyor, I was relieved after it passed inspection without incident. I then followed the crowd through Customs and then to the baggage claim area.

Seeing my luggage on the carousel was always a huge relief. This time, I felt even more relieved, since I had one bag that was packed with two cordless drill kits and other tools needed to finish the bridge's construction. I took a quick peek. As far as I could tell, nothing appeared to be missing. Walking through the crowded airport with all of those bags wasn't easy, but it was something I was willing to endure.

Finally getting to where the people were waiting to meet their loved ones, I heard a familiar voice, "THOMAS." It was Danilo! We quickly exchanged greetings and a firm handshake. He surprised me with the amount of English he knew; we were able to actually have a meaningful conversation about the bridge.

I followed Danilo outside the airport to a waiting pickup truck. I was expecting to see his van, so I questioned him about the truck. He said the *Alcaldía* of Matiguas had sent the truck to pick me up. I was immediately humbled, knowing the cost of the fuel and the driver was being provided by the town of Matiguas. After I got into the truck, Danilo once again thanked me for coming and informed me that he wouldn't be travelling back to Matiguas until Thursday.

I already knew from a previous e-mail that Milosz wouldn't arrive at the bridge site until Wednesday, but Danilo not being in Matiguas until Thursday was *not* what I needed to hear. This meant I would now be relying on my own language skills for securing the motel room and ride to the construction site each day. As we drove off I remembered thinking, *People must think I'm crazy for doing this . . . maybe I am.* Putting that thought aside, I took out my phone and called Cynthia to let her know I had arrived safely and was on the way to Matiguas. She was glad to hear from me and hoped that I would get a lot done.

After about thirty minutes on the road, I remembered a stop Mike would always make. I quickly pulled out my Spanish-English Dictionary and looked up the Spanish word for "banana." As soon as I had pronounced "*plátano*" to the driver, I looked up and saw the fresh market. I immediately pointed and excitedly shouted, "*Alto, Alto*!" The driver slowed down and pulled into the market, driving to where they sold bananas.

I got out of the truck and approached the produce stand. They seemed to sell almost every kind of fruit and vegetable you could imagine. Then I saw them—two boxes of the sweet, finger-sized bananas. Wanting to make sure I purchased the best tasting bunch, I grabbed and peeled one from the bunch that was on top. As I took the first bite, my mouth immediately turned inside-out, like after sucking on a piece of sour apple candy. I immediately spit it out. The produce lady laughed and pointed to a riper bunch. I peeled one and slowly took a bite. Though it smelled sweeter, all I could taste was the sour that still lingered in my mouth. But smelling the sweet aroma, I knew this was a good bunch. I bought the entire bunch for *veinte córdobas*, or about a dollar. As we were leaving, I almost felt like I was stealing, since I knew these ten bananas in the States would have cost over twice that amount.

We weren't even a mile down the road, and I had already eaten two bananas and shared one with the driver. Usually I only eat one, because Mike is the one who always buys them. But this time it was my turn to do the buying and the sharing.

It didn't seem very long before I woke up from my nap, feeling the bumpiness of the dirt road leading to Matiguas. I can't recall the reason, but there are several miles of the mountain road that are not paved. I knew that once the road became paved, we would only be about forty minutes from the town of Matiguas.

When we finally made it into town, it was dark, as usual. Thankfully, Danilo had instructed the driver to take me to the same motel that I stayed at in February. Upon entering the motel's lobby, I immediately recognized the owners, a young couple with a small baby. They also remembered me from my previous stay.

The woman was very patient at my attempt to communicate how many room nights I would need. I watched as she marked the days on a small scheduling calendar. Then she handed me the key. It was the same room as last time—room 13. The room number didn't bother me because I'm not at all superstitious. I was just thankful it had an air conditioner and a hot shower.

CHAPTER TWENTY-FIVE

A Bridge of Hope

I slept hard that first night and woke up early Sunday morning to send Cynthia a *Happy Mother's Day* e-mail. The e-mail included a picture of the television cart I had ordered for our bedroom, including where to pick it up. It wasn't the most romantic way of saying "Happy Mother's Day," but it was the best I could do from Nicaragua.

I sat in bed that morning reading in the book I had brought for the trip, *Build a Bridge and Get Over It!* I was starting the next chapter when my phone beeped. It was an e-mail from Cynthia thanking me for the Mother's Day gift, followed by the unforgettable words, "We don't have any water." *Oh no,* I thought, *she will never let me live this down—out of the country on Mother's Day and they have no running water.*

I immediately knew the "Dad's Our Mr. Fix-It" statement on my cartoon sweatshirt and my reputation of being able to fix anything now hung in the balance. I pondered several possible causes and after theoretically ruling out the well's pump, I knew the probable cause. My instructions to Cynthia needed to be concise because the average rate to call the States was two dollars per minute.

As soon as Cynthia answered the phone I tried to be positive by telling her "Happy Mother's Day," but I could tell by the tone of her voice those words weren't really what she wanted to hear. She told me she had already checked the breaker box and the breaker for the well wasn't tripped. This was good information to know, because if the well's motor had ran all night, it could have overheated and tripped the breaker. I then told her to go to Jordan's bathroom and lift the lid off the toilet's holding tank to see if it was empty, and if it was, to turn off the toilet's water valve. I confessed to her that was the only toilet in the house for which I had not changed the flapper valve in the holding tank. I was relieved when she e-mailed to tell me the flapper valve was the problem and that the water pressure at the sinks and showers was slowly increasing.

After enjoying that little bit of drama, it was time to go and enjoy a good hot breakfast. I quickly got dressed and headed out the door, grabbing the remaining bananas on the way out. Thankfully, Danilo's wife's café is only a short walking distance up the street from the motel.

The café is located on a street corner across from the town square, which means the streets stay really busy. I always enjoyed sitting outside on the patio, watching vehicles and people as they passed by—most of them as they stared at me. This morning as I sat and enjoyed a plate of scrambled eggs and ham, I held out a banana for each passing boy or girl. I loved seeing the smile come on their face as they took the small banana from my outstretched hand.

I then watched as a taxi driver drove up and went into the café. When he came out, I stopped him. Once I was comfortable he understood the location of the road to turn on that would take me to the Bulbul River, we agreed on a fare. I quickly finished my breakfast and got into his small car. We first stopped by the motel so I could get my backpack and the large duffle bag packed with the construction tools. I needed to get the construction tools to the small house where they could be secured with the other tools.

Riding down the long dirt road to the bridge site, I wasn't really sure if anyone would be there on a Sunday. In a previous e-mail, Milosz informed me that the daily volunteer labor from the communities had dwindled. But my real concern came when he mentioned that some days, the only workers were Carlos and Santos.

I remember sending an e-mail to Ken, expressing my concern that the community had seemingly given up on building the bridge, and my uncertainty about what I needed to do. He had a very insightful reply, "Thomas, it is not unusual for the community to lose its energy. Living in poverty one's whole life does that to you. You get beat down so many times, it gets harder and harder to get up." After I read his reply, I knew this would be a tangible purpose for my trip, for it to serve as a morale booster. I needed to work beside these communities for a week so they would still know I fully shared in their vision for the bridge.

I knew one way to encourage the two communities was to bring them gifts. In my duffle bag were a dozen hats, donated by a farming supply store, and a grocery bag filled with small packages of Easter candy that had been marked down to a quarter each. I planned to give the hats to the adult workers and the candy to the children. I believed demonstrating these simple acts of kindness would go a long way in motivating the two communities to complete their bridge.

Arriving at the bridge site, I saw in the distance a beautiful picture—the completed bridge tiers, cable towers, and walls of the approach ramp. It was a magnificent structure. I quickly walked down the hill to get a closer look. The stone tiers were enormous. It appeared to be almost fifteen feet to the top of the cable towers. Actually seeing the enormity of the construction reminded me of the great pyramids.

I carefully walked up the walls of the approach ramp to the top of the tiers and stood between the two cable towers. As I looked across the river to the other completed bridge tiers, I realized a Bridge of Hope, the dream of the people, was closer to becoming a reality. These two communities had come together to build something that was going to change not only their lives, but the lives of their children and grandchildren.

Santos had now gotten word that I had arrived and had come across the river to greet me. I smiled as we shook hands and indicated he had done a great job. We walked up to the house where the taxi driver had unloaded my bags. I unpacked each item from the duffle bag, showing Santos the two drill kits, the special wood bits, the rope, the box of hats, the bag of candy, the safety lanyards, and other miscellaneous items. Santos had a key to the storage room at the small house, so we placed everything inside. It eased my mind to know all of this was now safely delivered and secured at the construction site.

By this time, the owner of the house had returned, so we showed him the new construction tools and other items. His eyes got really big when I showed him the bag of candy, until I said, "*Para los niños*," or "For the children." But because he was allowing for the construction tools and bags of cement to be stored at his house, I gave him a brand new pair of orange coveralls and a hat as an appreciation gift.

Santos and I then walked over to the other side of the river so I could inspect the other stone tiers. I walked up the wall of the approach ramp and stood between the cable towers. Looking down across the river to the cable towers on the other side, I quickly spotted two tree limbs that would interfere with the bridge's handrail cables. Cutting the limbs would require someone to climb into the tree, but was something that could be done tomorrow.

With nothing else left to do, I decided it was time for me to head back into town and have some lunch. I shook Santo's hand and told him, "*Mañana*," or "Tomorrow." Then I realized there was one problem . . . I didn't have a ride back to town. I knew it was almost four miles to town, but with no other available options, I started walking.

Continuing to walk and gaze at the beautiful mountains, I thought to myself, *Here I am, walking on a long dirt road—in the middle of nowhere—in a third world country—alone . . . I* am *crazy.* I suddenly felt a great peace come over my whole body and fill my heart. I knew why I was sent here. This project had already taught me so much about not only myself but about faith.

At that moment, I heard something . . . a motorcycle. After passing by me, it suddenly stopped. I turned around and saw the rider stepping off. He had on a dirty baseball uniform and looked tired from playing a game. He motioned for me to come and get on. I shook my head and said "no" several times, knowing his house had to be at least two miles away on the other side of the river. He refused to get back on the motorcycle and, after speaking to the driver, started walking towards the river. I was really touched at his selflessness.

Riding on the back of the motorcycle, I began to realize that as I was walking, God was walking right beside me. Looking over at the mountains, I began to piece together the words to describe this incredible journey. And as we neared the end of the dirt road, I realized my life's journey would one day end, too. In the end, would I be asking myself if I had done enough to help others?

The Journey

Though the road before me
May now be dusty and long,
I know You walk beside me
So I do not walk alone.

Leading, guiding, protecting
Lighting the path ahead,
Sending, showing, providing
Walking on Faith, whatever lies ahead.

Though one day I know
The road will reach its end,
And I will glance back and say,
"Lord, thank You for the journey."

CHAPTER TWENTY-SIX

The Cables Arrive—Don't Quit Now

Monday was a day full of unknowns. These unknowns included not knowing when the delivery truck with the cables would arrive, the weight of each spool of cable, and how we could safely unload the spools. The only information from Milosz was that the truck would be delivering two big spools today: a spool of 7/8" steel cable and a spool of 1" steel cable. His e-mail also included detailed instructions on how to measure and cut each cable, and the order for pulling them across the river.

While the others talked and waited for the truck, I walked down to where the bridge's wooden crossbeams (which are placed across the walkway cables) and walking planks (which are nailed end-to-end between the crossbeams) were stacked. In his e-mail, Milosz had stated, "The planks that are there all need to be cut to 2 meters. They are now about 2.1 to 2.2 meters, and cut at a diagonal. We need to square off this diagonal, and get the planks to exactly 2 meters."

I looked up and saw that Carlos and Santos had followed me, probably to see if they could help with anything. I picked up the plank I had just finished marking and told them "*doscientos*." I showed them both ends had been cut at a slight diagonal and demonstrated how to use the carpentry square to mark a straight line to square the best end, then to measure 200 centimeters from that line and, using the carpentry square, draw a straight cutting line at the measured mark. Luckily for this plank, the best end was straight enough not to warrant cutting it a second time, though I still showed how to square the end. I gave Santos a pencil, and we all began measuring and marking the planks.

I hadn't turned around two seconds before Santos was tapping me on the shoulder. He pointed to the plank I had just marked and made a sign indicating my measurement was wrong. Carlos smiled as he proudly stretched his tape measure across the length of the plank. Santos pointed to where the tape measure crossed the line. I at first read it and said, "*Doscientos-cuatro*," which was 204. Santos quickly corrected me. I looked again, seeing it was 200.4 centimeters.

Knowing I had been more precise, I re-measured the plank with my tape measure. I showed them between the end and the mark was exactly *doscientos* on my ruler. Carlos and Santos both stood there for a moment with a confused look on their faces. I inconspicuously inspected the metal end on my tape measure to see if it was loose—it wasn't. Then I pointed for Carlos to hand me his tape measure. I immediately saw its end was bent outward, probably enough to add the 0.4 centimeters to his measurement. I showed Carlos the problem with his tape measure, and used the pliers on my multi-tool knife to straighten it. Carlos re-measured the plank—this time Santos gave me the thumbs-up sign.

After a couple of hours of marking and re-stacking the planks, it was time for a break. We walked up the hill to the house, where the other men were still waiting for the delivery truck. I noticed one of the teenagers had been to town and brought back a large soda and was now handing out sandwich bags and straws. He handed me a straw and a bag, and then filled it with soda. I smiled, since this was also how the soda was shared at the El Charcon bridge site in El Salvador. The store where the soda was purchased would usually provide the bags and the straws. With all of the workers now gathered around drinking soda, I took this opportunity to pass out the hats I had brought for them. They loved the new hats.

Soon after lunch, I heard the rumbling sound of an approaching truck. Everyone cheered as the truck drove up—it was the delivery truck carrying the spools of cable. Within minutes, several of the men were helping the driver back the truck down the hill towards the construction area. The truck was stopped just short of the large pile of gravel. It appeared the plan was to allow each spool to free-fall the four feet from the back of the truck onto the ground, with the pile of gravel to act as a stop for the rolling spool.

After the driver had fully opened the rollup door, several of the men jumped into the back and started trying to move one of the spools. They couldn't; the spool was blocked with several short pieces of cut lumber nailed to the truck's decking. After the driver used his hammer to remove those pieces, the men slowly rolled the first spool of cable to the back of the truck. With one final push, the spool fell from the truck and slammed to the ground, causing the earth to tremble underneath my feet. They unloaded the second spool in a similar manner.

Each spool of cable was so heavy that when it landed on the ground, it only rolled a few feet. We were fortunate that the wooden spools appeared to have been stored inside of a warehouse, since they were both in great condition. Otherwise, when the spool hit the ground, it would have broken apart, making a giant mess. As heavy as they were, I was really just thankful no one had gotten hurt unloading them.

While everyone marveled at how large the cables were, I got my gloves, hammer and screwdriver from my backpack. I went to the spool with the 1" cable and, with a few of the other men, pushed the spool onto its side. After locating the cable's end, I showed Carlos where to place his foot on the cable. I was merely being cautious of the end's recoil, since I couldn't tell how tight the cable had been wrapped around the spool. After a little effort, I pried free the large staple securing the cable's end to the spool. I motioned for Carlos to slowly remove his foot from the cable. To my surprise, the end didn't move much. I then went and removed the staple from the 7/8" cable spool.

It was still early in the afternoon, so I made the decision to pull the 1" cable off the spool. I made it my job to unspool the cable, which meant unwinding the cable from around the spool and in the same motion, pulling it up and over the top of the spool at the back. As I grabbed hold of the cable's end, I immediately realized it was very stiff, greasy, and really heavy.

Once I had several meters of the cable unspooled, all of the other men started grabbing onto the greasy cable, some using the available gloves and others using torn paper from the cement bags. At first, they spaced themselves too closely together, but after realizing the heaviness of the steel cable, spread out more. This made it easier for everyone to carry as the train of men slowly walked the cable up the hill towards the road.

After each turn, I hollered for the men to pull. Often they would pull too much, so Santos and I would have to grab and pull the whole run of cable back towards the spool so that I could gain enough slack to unspool another turn of the cable. After almost thirty minutes, I had to stop. At that moment I remember thinking, *This is more physically demanding than carrying stones.*

Since we had stopped for a break, Carlos walked down the hill to where I was sitting, taking a drink of lukewarm water and eating a snack. He was holding the tape measure and pointed back at the cable lying on the ground. I took one more drink of water and we both walked over to the cable. Santos came over to see what we were doing. I gave Santos the end of the tape and pointed up the hill, then stated to Carlos, "*Ciento veinte y dos metros*," which translates to 122 meters, or 400 feet. (Note: It was 214 feet between the bridge tiers and an average of 43 feet down each approach ramp to the cable anchor, with another 50 feet needed to wrap the cable around each anchor.)

Once I saw Santos had stopped walking, I looked down and read the tape measure—it was about 87 meters, or 285 feet. By the exhausted looks already on everyone's face, I wasn't sure if we had enough help to even get this first 122 meters of cable pulled out. But more importantly, I didn't know how much help we were going to need tomorrow to pull each cable across the river and up the twenty-foot cliff on the other side. To me, these cables were going to be the ultimate test for these two communities.

Taking my position back at the cable spool, I watched as all of the men resumed their position along the cable. We worked for another fifteen minutes before stopping to re-measure the length of the cable. This time, it measured 120 meters, meaning only a couple of more turns were needed . . . for this first run of cable. However, two more 122-meter pulls were needed from this spool, since the bridge design now called for three 1" cables—one for each handrail and one in the center of the walking platform.

We pulled a little extra cable from the spool before we rechecked the measurement. We made sure the tape measure was placed directly beside the cable for its entire length. Once we were comfortable with the 122-meter mark, we prepared the cable for cutting. Thankfully, Milosz had included cable cutting instructions in his e-mail sent a few days before I left. After reading over them, I had gone and purchased a pair of cutting pliers and a small roll of steel tie wire.

Per Milosz's instructions, I cut a small piece of the tie wire and wrapped it once around the cable, then tightly twisted the ends together with my pliers. Since I had a full roll, I installed two pieces of tie wire on each side of the cut mark, just in case one broke during the cutting of the cable—I wasn't taking any chances of the cable fraying after it was cut.

Satisfied I had installed the tie wires correctly, I got the hacksaw and installed one of the new blades. Starting to saw on the steel cable, I noticed the blade was merely making a scratch. I tried again, this time putting more pressure on the saw. After several additional strokes, I looked again at the cable—this apparently was not going to work.

Santos tapped me on the shoulder and indicated for me to follow him up to the small house. Once inside the house, he reached into a five-gallon bucket and brought out a small electric side grinder and a pair of gloves. Thinking back, Milosz had mentioned in his e-mail something about cutting the cable with a side grinder. The only problem was, this house had no electricity.

Santos read the question mark on my face and did a great job in conveying that the *Alcaldía* would be bringing a generator tomorrow morning. In fact, after I reviewed Milosz's e-mail on my phone, he had included this bit of information. But an immediate problem I now saw was that the cutting disk on the grinder was really worn, and there weren't any more disks in the bucket. Solving one problem always seemed to lead to another.

With the question of how we were going to cut the steel cable now answered, Santos and I went back to where the other men were waiting. I signaled for everyone to come back and start dragging out a run of the 7/8" cable. I knew we couldn't cut the cables until we got the generator, but I wanted to take full advantage of the number of men who were now helping. After finishing this backbreaking work today, I wasn't sure how many would return to help with the cables tomorrow.

I grabbed the cable's end, quickly unspooled several meters, and handed the end to the man standing closest to me. He took hold of it and started walking up the hill. As fast as I could unspool the cable, there was a man standing in front of me, ready to grab hold and carry it. It wasn't long before everyone was helping carry the cable. Even the younger teenagers were starting to help.

Each time I would unspool this smaller diameter cable, it kept trying to kink in front of the spool. Banking on my utility experience, I motioned for everyone to untwist the cable as they pulled it. This action would prevent the cable from kinking, or tying itself into a knot. When the men didn't do this, I would grab the cable as a kink tried to form and force the cable to untwist.

At some point, I became exhausted and let a younger man take over the unspooling of the cable. I grabbed my bottled water and sat down near the cable spool, watching to make sure he was observing the cable as the men pulled it. The next moment, I heard him holler to the others. I looked up and saw the kink in the cable. I jumped to my feet and hollered "*Alto*!" but I was one second too late. There were so many men carrying and pulling on the cable that they actually pulled the steel cable "through" the kink, which means the cable had straightened itself back out. And no, . . . this is *not* a good thing.

I showed the two men closest to the cable spool the irreversible damage caused by the kink, a direct result of not untwisting the cable as it was unspooled. There was nothing to do except finish pulling out the cable until they reached the end of the 1" cable, which would signify 122 meters. For the next twenty minutes, I unspooled the cable, letting the men make a small pull, and at the same time watching for any kinks that would try to form.

The unspooling of the 7/8" cable went much smoother and a little bit faster. But after standing in one spot for so long, I could hardly manage to walk. Not only that, my arms felt like spaghetti. Fortunately, the work was done for the day.

Before leaving, I went and inspected the 7/8" cable where it had kinked. The cable was badly damaged—six of the small steel strands of the cable had actually broken in two. The cable would have to be cut before this damaged area, which meant the remaining portion would be scrapped. So much effort and time wasted because of my inattention and inability to fully communicate with these men.

Later, at Danilo's aunt's restaurant, I sat and ate in solitude. I was physically exhausted beyond what my body had ever experienced. Not only that, having to tell those men tomorrow that a portion of the cable we unspooled would be scrapped. What would they think about that? And with so much effort required just to unspool the cable, how would we pull the cables up that rock wall—which was basically a vertical cliff?

As I finished eating what I could of the baked chicken, rice, and beans, I thought about Milosz. He knew how physically demanding the unspooling of those heavy steel cables would be. When pulling them across the river, he also saw the obstacle of the rock wall. Maybe this was his litmus test for me . . . to see if I was up for the challenge. If that was it, he had won. This work was too demanding for even me.

That night in bed, I typed Cynthia a short e-mail. I told her that handling the steel cables was extremely physically demanding work, beyond what I was capable of doing, and I was ready to quit and come home. And the thought of when I tell people the story of the ten one-dollar bills—of how God was there at a simple car wash fundraiser; what would I tell them when they asked if I had ever felt God's presence at the bridge site in Nicaragua? My answer would have to be a "no." Even though I knew beyond any doubt I was called by God to build this bridge, I had never experienced anything that I could honestly say "God did that."

I didn't get a reply from Cynthia until early Tuesday morning. Her e-mail message was very direct, "Thomas, you can't quit . . . you've come too far to quit now." *Well,* I thought, *at least my wife believes I can build this bridge.* But she didn't have any idea of the physical condition of my body. I was well rested, but still really sore. There was simply no way I could work another day handling those heavy steel cables.

As I continued to lie in bed, thinking of my options, I said a short prayer, "Lord, You've brought me this far, and now I'm ready to give up. What do You want me to do? I need an answer." Then I sat up and re-read Cynthia's e-mail. It was at least comforting to know *she* believed in me.

I reached for the book *Build a Bridge and Get Over It!* I still had the last chapter to read and thought, *If I'm going home today, I might as well be able to say that I had finished something.* Strangely, the bookmark was still marking Chapter 7. I quickly turned the pages to the beginning of Chapter 8 and stopped and stared in almost disbelief at the chapter's title. I was stunned, for right there before my very eyes, the answer to my prayer:—*DON'T QUIT NOW.* I know without a doubt this was God's answer to my prayer. Not only that, He even provided me the motivation I needed with the last statement in the book, "The bridge of perseverance is the hardest to erect, but the most rewarding to cross."

CHAPTER TWENTY-SEVEN

God Moved

Don't quit now. With that answer, I started thinking of a way to get those cables up that twenty-foot rock wall. But with only a handful of tools and resources available at the bridge site, was there a simple solution?

Then I remembered the rope I had brought to secure the cables. I could tie a small rock on one end and throw it over the edge. The men at the bottom would tie the rope around the cable; and then a few other men and I would pull the cable to the top of the cliff. In my mind, this seemed like it would work.

At the bridge site I was relieved to see most of the men had returned to help. I had already seen a few of the other men standing along the roadside with their canisters of fresh milk, waiting for the truck to come by and collect it. Though these two communities needed a bridge, they still had to do what was necessary to provide for their families each day.

The first thing I did that morning was place a piece of red flagging tape around the damaged area of the 7/8" cable. This would be the first place to be cut, because I wasn't taking any chances of this damaged section getting pulled across the river. Unfortunately, I knew this meant there wouldn't be enough of the 7/8" cable left for all the needed pulls this week.

Still waiting on the generator, I went to the small house and retrieved the grinder, leather gloves, face shield, and small roll of tie wire. I walked back to where the damaged piece of cable needed to be cut. I cut and wrapped a small piece of the tie wire around the cable, then tightly twisted the ends together with my pliers. Just like on the 1" cable, I installed two pieces of tie wire on each side of the cut mark.

It wasn't long before the truck carrying the generator arrived. I was glad to see the generator was equipped with wheels on one end, since I knew there weren't any extension cords readily available. The only problem with the generator was that it apparently didn't get used much, because at first it wouldn't crank. I stood back as several of the men, including Santos and Carlos, worked on it. After about thirty minutes of them tinkering with the carburetor and spark plug, it finally cranked. We let it continue to run while we maneuvered it down the hill to the cable.

Being in a developing country, I wasn't sure how many of these men had ever used a side grinder. I knew this type of grinder, with its thin rotating cutting disk, is a power tool that deserved its rightful respect. One slip while cutting and you could easily come up missing a finger or two. Being the safety coordinator at the electric company, I knew to don all of the necessary safety equipment, including wearing a long sleeve shirt, leather gloves, and face shield to protect myself from the hot sparks created as the cable was being cut.

I placed a small piece of wood under the cable, lifting it slightly off the ground. I signaled for two men to stand on each side of the cut mark and place a foot on the cable—to keep the cable from moving while it was being cut. With the preparation work completed, I plugged in the grinder. I flipped on the generator's circuit breaker and slowly pressed on the grinder's large trigger. I wasn't surprised that the grinder sounded just like the one I used at home, with its thin cutting disk spinning at several thousand revolutions per minute.

I carefully turned the grinder sideways and placed the rotating disk on the cut mark. As I watched the spinning disk eating its way through the 7/8" steel cable, I noticed the disk not only glowed bright red, but got a lot smaller too. As I finished the cut, I let go of the grinder's trigger and held it up in the sunlight. Everyone who saw it immediately began laughing. Now I knew what my dad meant when he would say, "Son, let the tool do the work," because only a small cutting area now remained on the disk. I had obviously rushed the cut.

While the other men were pulling the generator and carrying the tools down the hill to the cable spools, Santos and I went back to the small house to look one more time for extra cutting disks. To our dismay, we still didn't find any. Then I thought, *What are the chances of finding these small cutting disks in a town of a third world country?* Building a bridge in a developing country, I had already learned to be resourceful, but the side grinder was the only way I saw to cut these large diameter steel cables.

Walking down the hill, I noticed the men had already unspooled more of the 7/8" cable. Carlos showed me the red flagging tape he had placed on the cable at the 122 meter mark. This made me remember that the Bridges to Prosperity's main objective and the main purpose for me coming and helping build this bridge was to show and train these communities—to make the building of these bridges sustainable. So this time, I placed and twisted two tie wires on one side of the cut mark, and let Carlos install the other two. As Carlos was making the final twist on his last tie, it broke. This was obviously the training part, or trial and error, since I had broken a few myself.

With the 7/8" cable now prepared for cutting, it was now time to make the second cut of the day. Carlos again had to pull on the rope several times before the generator would crank, but once it did, it idled smoothly. I put on the gloves and face shield, and began cutting into the 7/8" cable. This time I went much slower, trying to preserve what cutting surface was left on the disk.

We then repeated the same cutting preparation steps for the 1" cable. As I finished cutting the cable, I could tell that was the last cut to be made with that disk. With no replacement disks available for cutting the remaining cables, our work was eventually going to come to a standstill. At that moment, a gentleman in a uniformed shirt rode up on a motorcycle and started talking with Santos. From what I could understand from the conversation, he wanted to make sure we were satisfied with the generator. Then Santos pointed at me.

As the man approached me, I immediately recognized the insignia on his shirt—he worked for the *Alcaldía*. Milosz had stated in an e-mail that officials from the *Alcaldía* had on several occasions met with the communities, trying to encourage them to continue working on the bridge. I wasn't surprised by the *Alcaldía*'s involvement, since I believed they knew if the communities failed to complete this bridge, then my church probably wouldn't provide the funding to build another one. In actuality, I knew if the communities failed to complete this bridge, then I would have a really difficult time raising the funds for another bridge. The successful completion of this first bridge was going to be a win-win for everyone involved.

After exchanging names and a handshake, I showed him the grinder's worn out cutting disk. Carlos came over and asked (what would have taken me a lot longer to ask) if he would go and purchase more cutting disks. He gave a positive response and a smile. Now the only problem I saw was in how to remove the worn out disk from the grinder.

The cutting disk is held firmly in place by a large, flat nut which has four narrow, equally spaced slots. I knew the only way to loosen and remove that nut was by placing a small blunt object, such as a common screwdriver, at the edge of one of those slots. Lightly tapping on the screwdriver with a hammer would cause the large nut to slowly rotate and loosen, allowing the removal of the disk. On my trips, I always brought a hammer but never saw the need for bringing a screwdriver, until now.

I went and began searching through my backpack, hoping by chance to find something that could be used in lieu of a screwdriver. I couldn't find anything to use except for a knife. Then I glanced over at the clear snack container and remembered what the security officer had found in it at the airport . . . a center punch. I smiled widely as I walked over and picked up the container, removed the lid, and pulled out the center punch.

It only took a couple of taps on the punch before the nut broke free. I quickly removed the nut and the cutting disk from the grinder. I wrapped the disk in a napkin before I handed it to the gentleman, telling him, "*Cuatro*," or "Four." "*Sí*," was his reply, holding out his hand to indicate he needed money. I reached and took out my wallet and discovered that I didn't have any Nicaraguan money to give him. There were a few American dollar bills, but I knew they wouldn't be enough to purchase even one disk.

Though I had never met this man before, I reached into my wallet and took out a brand new, one hundred-dollar bill. The look of amazement on his face was priceless as I handed the bill to him. This was probably more than he normally made in a week at his job. Still, I had complete trust and faith that he would return before lunch with the four cutting disks and my change.

Putting those thoughts aside, I took my position in front of the 7/8" cable spool and started the routine of unspooling and watching for any kinks that tried to form. When the men finally stopped pulling, I knew they had to be close to where they had stopped with the other cables. I quickly looked up and at that moment became a little light-headed. I could see that Carlos was waiting up the hill with the tape measure, but I was too exhausted to even take two steps. I paused for a moment, then leaned and placed my head down on the cable spool. I closed my eyes, trying to physically dig deeper . . . trying to muster another ounce of strength.

The next thing I remember was being startled by the crashing sound of a plastic bag that dropped on the spool near my head. I opened my eyes enough to tell the bag contained the four cutting disks that we desperately needed. I quickly looked up and saw the gentleman from the *Alcaldía* smiling while holding a wad of bills. I stood up straight and held out my hand, listening as he counted each bill . . . then the coins. Honestly, at that moment, I couldn't have told you if he gave me back the right amount of change or not. I smiled and stuffed the money in my pants' pocket, because in my heart, I knew he had. There was no reason for him to try and keep any of the money, since he already knew how much of my own time and my church's money had been given to his people and this project.

I looked over and noticed that one of the men had already placed a new disk on the shaft of the grinder. He had apparently watched me remove the old disk that morning. I watched as he finished tightening the large nut using the hammer and center punch. He actually did a good job in tightening the nut.

After he handed me the grinder I tried to give the new disk a test spin, but it wouldn't turn. I knew the disk was the correct size. I turned the grinder over and saw he had simply installed the disk upside down. An innocent mistake, but one that could have damaged the grinder's motor when it was turned on. I got the hammer and punch and removed the disk, flipped it over, and re-installed it. This time, the disk spun freely. I made sure Carlos was watching me correctly install and check the disk, since he would probably be doing the next one.

After preparing the 7/8" cable to be cut, I stepped over to the 1" cable spool and once again began the unspooling process. Thankfully, more men had now shown up to help with this heavier cable. Once the signal was given to stop pulling, the cable was measured and marked at 122 meters. This time, I let Carlos prepare the cable for cutting. He confidently demonstrated that he knew what he was doing.

When Carlos had finished, he placed a piece of wood under the cable and had two guys stand on the cable. He cranked the generator and plugged the grinder's cord into the 120 volt outlet. He put on the face shield and made a slow, smooth cut through the 1" cable. Then he moved to the other side of the generator and cut the 7/8" cable.

With all the cables now cut, we started the unspooling of the remaining 7/8" cable. I let two other men manage the unspooling of the cable. There were only a few wraps of cable left on the spool when I grabbed the cable to help pull it up the hill. Once all the cable was pulled off the spool, I hollered, "*Alto*!" signaling for everyone to stop pulling. Then I noticed something—a welded cable splice. I reluctantly took a picture and e-mailed it to Milosz, all the time knowing a length of cable with any type of splice couldn't be used for the pedestrian bridge.

Then something totally unexpected happened—it began to pour down rain. Everyone scrambled for the little shelter available underneath the trees. I ran and grabbed my backpack, then took refuge in the empty cable spool. As it continued to rain, I noticed Santos, Gary, and the gentleman from the *Alcaldía* all standing against the bridge tiers—which offered them no shelter. They were standing there getting soaking wet.

Suddenly, something moved on the opposite side of the cable spool. I slowly peeked around the center of the wooden spool, expecting to see a man contortioned somewhat like me. Instead I came face-to-face with . . . A DOG! I let out a screech, but the dog didn't move. I laughed, thinking this was probably the best dog house he had ever been in—one where he actually didn't get wet inside.

As I repositioned myself to avoid the water starting to drip from the top of the cable spool, I looked over at the men who were still standing against the bridge tiers. Now getting wetter from the blowing rain, I remembered the poncho in my backpack. Finding the poncho, I thought for a moment . . . then ran and gave it to the gentleman from the *Alcaldía*. After all, it was the *Alcaldía* who had sent the air conditioned truck to pick me up at the airport and provided the generator.

The rain lasted well over thirty minutes before finally tapering off. I quickly tied a piece of red flagging tape to mark each cable's center and placed a designated color of electrical tape on each of the ends. The flagging tape at the center was so that the excess cable for the cable anchors could be divided equally between the two sides without having to guess.

Now turning my attention back to the cables, I knew we had two 7/8" and two 1" cables that were ready to be pulled across the river. Getting the attention of Santos and Gary, I pointed to the cables and then to the other side of the river. Gary, the Patastule community leader, stood at the end of the 1" cable and yelled for everyone to grab hold of it. I watched as each man picked up the huge cable and slowly started walking it down the steep bank towards the river.

They didn't stop at the river, but instead waded across it and stopped on the other side at the bottom of the twenty-foot cliff. A few of the men stood in the middle of the river, keeping the cable out of the water. The river at this location was only about fifteen feet across and maybe three feet deep. Thankfully, the winter rains had not yet poured down in this region of the mountains.

Seeing the men stop at the bottom of the rock wall, I hurried to my backpack. I quickly took out several pieces of the rope and ran across the large stones in the river to the other side. I picked up a small stone, tied it on the end of the rope, and slowly lowered it over the edge of the cliff. Once the rope reached the men below one man grabbed it, removed the stone, and tied the rope around the cable. Then he signaled for me to start pulling the rope back.

With more men now helping pull the 1" cable up the rock wall, I walked around the bridge tiers and located a tree to affix the cable. I wrapped a piece of rope around a tree and tied several knots to secure it. As the men were carrying the cable towards me, I made one hand-cuff type hitch and placed it over the end of the cable. I motioned for them to keep pulling as I quickly placed two more hitches on the cable.

No sooner was the 1" cable secured than the men had starting hoisting up the 7/8" cable. I quickly demonstrated to Carlos that this cable needed to be brought to the top of the bridge tiers and taken between the cable towers. The men then followed me down the approach ramp to the cable anchor, which at this point was a ten-foot hole in the ground.

We needed to secure this walkway cable to one of the trees behind the cable anchor. The only problem with accessing these trees was that the anchor excavation's spoil pile, a sizable mound of shale rock, lay between the excavation and the trees. I placed three hand-cuff hitches on the cable and threw the rope across the excavation to Carlos. Standing on the rocks, Carlos reached and tied the rope around a tree. Although it was the largest tree he could reach, I knew it would easily pull over when the cable was pulled tight from the other side.

I carefully crept down the backside of the mound of rock, but still slipped and slid most of the way. I stopped at the bottom of the largest tree. With the other men pulling on the cable, Carlos untied the rope from the tree and slung it towards me. I grabbed the rope and secured it at the bottom of a larger tree. With both cables now secured, everyone went to the other side to secure the other ends.

On this side of the river there was only one tree in the hayfield behind the cable anchor excavation. Though the tree was over fifty feet away, it was perfectly in-line with the approach ramp. I wrapped a longer piece of rope around the tree and tied several knots to secure it, then waited for the cable.

I got excited as the first two men pulling the 7/8" cable emerged at the top of the bridge tiers. I could already tell they were struggling with the cable as they began walking down the approach ramp wall. With the help of five others, the cable was carried around the anchor excavation and towards the tree where Santos and I were waiting with the rope.

When the tension on the cable became too great for them to pull any more, the men stopped. The cable was almost within my reach. At that moment, I shouted, "*Uno . . . Dos . . . Tres*," and they pulled the cable another meter. Santos and I hurriedly slipped one hitch on the end of the cable. Then I helplessly watched as the cable began slipping back through the single hitch. We simply had to pull more cable across.

With a look of desperation I shouted at Santos, "*Tres*! *Tres*!" I let Santos hold the rope so Carlos and I could both help the men pull. This time, I cried out, "*UNO . . . DOS . . . TRES*!" With all nine of us pulling as one, the cable moved just enough to allow Santos to place two more hitches around it. Everyone relaxed for a moment.

Then we pulled and routed the 1" cable around the bridge tiers, securing it to the same tree. This 1" cable was one of the bridge's handrail cables and would later be placed on top of the cable tower. With both cables now sagging high above the river, everyone took a well-deserved break.

During the break, Carlos noticed that the 7/8" cable was slowly slipping through the three hitches. He pointed to the cable, indicating to me that it was very greasy. I had a small roll of electrical tape in my pocket, so I tightly wrapped a piece in front of each hitch. The cable stopped moving. Then Carlos frantically pointed to the cables on the other side of the river and immediately grabbed the tape from my hand. I knew exactly what he was going to do.

Standing between the cable towers, I was relieved to see Carlos as he emerged from behind the far-side bridge tiers. The hitches placed on those cables seemed to be holding, but I felt more at ease with the wraps of tape on them. I stood for another minute and watched the other men looking at the two cables sagging across the river. I could tell they were excited at what they had accomplished.

I broke the silence with, "Hey . . . cable." Even though it was an enjoyable moment for everyone, we still had two more runs of cable to pull across the river. We spent the next hour pulling the remaining 7/8" and 1" cables across the river and securing them with additional pieces of rope. Unfortunately, there wasn't enough of the 1" cable left on the spool for another full pull, so the day ended with only four cables being pulled across the river.

On Wednesday, we worked on cutting the walking planks to the proper length. Everyone took a turn using the wooden handled handsaw, which had a large flimsy cutting blade like the one I inherited from my grandfather. Though I hated using that saw, I made sure to take my fair share of turns with this one, since there were well over a hundred boards to be cut.

That afternoon, Milosz came to the bridge site to inspect our progress. He surprised me with the bridge plaques he had made in El Salvador—one in Spanish to place on the bridge and one in English to display in my church. The golden metal plaques with black engraved lettering were absolutely beautiful in the bright sunshine. I read and reflected upon each name, but stopped to point out Orlando's name to Santos.

After Milosz had finished inspecting the cables, he dictated a long to-do list to me. The main task was to cut a thirty meter roll of tubing into six smaller pieces, then wrap and tie each piece around the near-side anchor's rebar cage. After placing the rebar cage into the excavation, each cable would be pushed through a tube and temporarily secured back to itself using a few cable clamps. All the materials we would need were stored inside the house at the top of the hill.

Before I could ask any questions, Milosz handed me a long nylon lifting sling from the back of his SUV. I listened carefully as he explained that the sling was to be placed around the cable towers to hold the tension of the cables while the ends were untied and fed through the tubes. When I asked him how I was to attach the cables to the sling, he sarcastically replied, "Figure it out, Thomas."

Then Milosz brought out a familiar looking tool and asked, "Do you think you can use this?" Smiling as I took the tool from him, I emphatically answered, "I believe so." The tool was a small handheld winch, commonly known as a come-along. I remembered as a kid watching my dad use one to tighten the chain link fence around the garden in Great Falls. I wasn't exactly sure how I was going to use it to attach the cables to the sling, but knew it could pull and tension each cable. It was now getting late and Milosz needed to leave, so we carried and locked everything inside the house.

We worked all Thursday morning cutting and securing the tubes around the rebar cage. After lunch, we maneuvered the cage into the excavation behind the approach ramp. This job ended up being much more difficult than it first appeared due to having to cut away the excess lengths of rebar on both ends with a hacksaw. Once the cage was squarely in place and at the correct angle, the twelve flexible tubing ends flared out of the anchor excavation like the tentacles of an octopus. I nicknamed it the "conduit monster" and took a quick picture. This was our only accomplishment for that day.

Friday morning at breakfast, I checked over Milosz's to-do list and read the last two items. The first remaining task was to attach the cables to the nylon sling so the ropes could be untied from the cables. The last task was to push each cable through a tube and secure the end of the cable with the cable clamps. I meticulously thought through the steps of each task and anything I needed to purchase.

Right off, I knew from my underground cable pulling experience at the electric company that coating the first couple of feet of the cable with a lubricant would make it easier to push through the tube. So before leaving I walked over to the small store located on the opposite street corner.

Inside the store reminded me a lot of the old pharmacy that once operated on the street corner in the part of my hometown known as Flopeye, but much smaller and a lot less convenient. It seemed that almost every item in this pharmacy was either behind the counter or in a glass display case. Behind the counters, there was shampoo, soap, hair products, diapers, toothpaste, and other baby care items, but nothing like petroleum jelly. The mob of people made it very difficult to peer into the display cases, but I looked the best I could twice.

I slowly walked outside to meet my ride. Before mounting the motorcycle, I decided to walk back into the store to take one last look. Most of the "standing room only" crowd had now dispersed, allowing me to get a closer look at the items in the display cases. Scanning over every product, my eyes grew wider when they spotted the small jars of petroleum jelly.

Arriving at the bridge site, I was encouraged at what I saw. Instead of sitting and waiting for me to tell them what to do, the men and women of the community were already busy cutting the boards for the walking planks. I took a few pictures and then showed Carlos and Santos the proper way to stack the boards to prevent them from warping, knowing they would be sitting out in the weather for at least another month.

Turning my attention to the real work that needed to get done today, I walked down and stepped over the approach wall to devise the best method of getting the cables fed through the tubes. Carlos walked back towards the tree, stopping where the ropes were tied to the cables. When I got to him, he already had out his pocket knife ready to cut the rope from one of the cables. Though this would be the easiest way, I politely discouraged him because I knew that today with only seven men, counting ourselves, pulling and tensioning the cable back across the river would be nearly impossible.

I went and stood in front of the bridge tiers and looked up at the three walkway cables lying between the cable towers. The fourth cable, designated as a handrail cable, was still lying on the ground beside the tiers. Santos soon returned with the come-along and nylon sling from the house. I took the sling and pointed to the cable towers. I watched as two men climbed up the tiers and placed the sling over the towers. The sling fully encircled both towers. I grabbed the come-along and snapped its stationary hook onto the sling, let out about a foot of its steel cable, and held its cable hook up beside the first 7/8" cable.

I watched as Carlos took a short piece of rebar and bent it into the shape of a hook. He held the rebar hook up to the 7/8" cable to show me his idea of attaching it to the cable. This was an excellent idea. I took and held the hook against the cable while Carlos attached it with several pieces of the steel tie wire. With the hook now secured to the cable, I stretched and snapped the come-along's cable hook onto it.

Then, I helped Carlos make a second hook from the rebar which we attached to the cable at a point about a foot from the sling. My idea was to pull a little more cable across with the come-along so that this second hook could be placed over the nylon sling. Once we removed the come-along, the sling would then be holding the full tension of the cable like we needed.

I slowly started winching the 7/8" cable towards me with the come-along. Each time after fully pulling the handle towards me, I would point to the come-along's mechanical brake, or ratchet lever, indicating I was making sure it was fully engaged before releasing and moving the handle back to the forward position. I knew the importance of that lever being fully engaged after each pull, and the consequences if the handle was released and it wasn't—the come-along would uncontrollably unwind a portion or even all of its cable.

After several repetitions with the come-along, I could already tell we had attached the second hook too far down on the cable. Regardless of that fact, I kept pulling the handle back, checking the ratchet lever, releasing the handle forward, and then pulling it back again. This was dangerous, and I became a little uneasy because I knew the small come-along was now transferring several tons of force between the rebar hook and the nylon sling.

The second hook was now almost touching the sling and with one more pull . . . *POW!* The distinctive sound of a rifle being fired caused everyone to immediately look up and across the river to where the sound originated. At that moment, everyone saw the 7/8" cable sliding off of the far-side bridge tier, and finally the end of the cable as it plummeted off the cliff—landing on the rocks below.

For a moment everyone just stood there in astonishment, no one wanting to believe what they had just witnessed. It became apparent that the rifle sound we heard was actually the pull-tape rope, stretched to almost its breaking point, finally slipping off the end of the cable and instantly recoiling.

Then I saw something incredible . . . one of the men had already made it across the river and was starting to climb the near vertical rock wall. He had the end of the cable in one hand and was somehow finding footholds and grabbing onto every vine that he could, pulling himself up that wall like a spider.

Some of the men ran and started helping him by pushing the cable up the wall, while others were now standing on top of the cliff waiting to grab the end of the cable. They were like a well trained army, following their commander. But who was the man scaling the wall? I quickly went down to the river to get a closer look.

It was Gary, the Patastule community leader, now leading his people in battle. He had probably seen too many people over his lifetime drown in that river. And then knowing his friend, Orlando, was the most recent victim. Gary knew that completing this bridge would forever end that cycle of tragedy for his people. He was determined to win the war.

Once they had re-secured the cable, everyone came back across to help with the next one. Carlos and I first inspected how the cables were tied off with the rope. We immediately noticed that even with three hand-cuff hitches and the added pieces of tape, the cables were still creeping back through. The large cables sagging across the river were not only heavy and greasy, but also under a lot of tension.

Carlos then demonstrated to me an idea of using the steel tie wire to better secure the rope to the cable. I nodded my head in agreement. He hurriedly went and got the reel of tie wire and the pliers. I watched as he wrapped and tightly twisted a small piece of the tie wire in front of each hand-cuff hitch.

After Carlos finished applying the three wraps of tie wire to each cable, he pointed towards the far-side bridge tiers. "*Sí*," was my immediate response to him. He left with a few of the others following close behind. Once they returned, we completed winching and attaching the second 7/8" walkway cable to the sling. Attaching the second cable went a lot faster because we had solved all of the pitfalls encountered with the first cable.

The 1" walkway cable and the 1" handrail cable still remained to be worked. With rain now threatening, I helped Carlos quickly secure the two rebar hooks to the 1" walkway cable. This was the last cable I wanted to get attached to the sling because I needed to get a few of the cables pulled through the ducts so I could show Santos and Carlos how to properly install the cable clamps.

Since this was my last day, I let Carlos operate the come-along for this cable. I showed him the ratchet lever and how to properly release the handle and move it back forward—in position for the next pull. After he completed a couple of pulling sequences with my instructions, I stepped back to let him complete the next pulling sequence on his own.

Carlos pulled the come-along's handle towards him very slowly and then inspected the ratchet lever before releasing and moving the handle back to the forward position. But his next pull was very quick and deliberate, and without checking to make sure the ratchet lever was fully engaged, he released the handle to move back forward. He quickly jumped back, letting go of the handle as the come-along uncontrollably unspooled over a foot of its cable. I again pointed to the ratchet lever.

It was now getting late, so I grabbed the handle and began rapidly operating the come-along, not stopping to give Carlos anymore instructions. I quickly completed several more pulling sequences with the come-along. As the men were struggling to get the second rebar hook placed on the sling . . . *POW!* The sound was unmistakable. Everyone briefly stopped and looked across the river to witness the 1" walkway cable slowly sliding over the bridge tier. At that moment, we all seemingly lowered our heads in defeat.

I was the first person to reach the far-side bridge tiers. I glanced over and saw the 1" handrail cable still secured and lying on the ground. Then I stood beside the bridge tiers and looked up and counted three cables still lying between the cable towers. I thought to myself, *The cable must have gotten caught on something.* This made perfect sense because I never saw the end of the cable come off the bridge tiers.

I carefully stepped around to the back of the bridge tiers, thinking one wrong move would cause the cable to dislodge from whatever it was caught on. Peeping over the approach wall, I saw the three walkway cables lying side by side, with the cable ends perfectly aligned with each other. To my astonishment, all three cables were each still secured to the tree with a piece of rope—the rope attached to the end of each cable with three hand-cuff hitches and steel tie wire in front of each hitch. For a moment I just stood there, not able to comprehend what I was seeing. What had just happened?

And the night at church when I gave the Nicaragua Mission Team's project update, as I finished telling this story, I slowly looked over the crowd of people in attendance and when I saw Bob staring at me . . . my eyes locked with his and I gave the answer: "Bob, . . . God moved."

AFTERWORD

LOVE THY NEIGHBOR

The bridge in Nicaragua was finished in July of 2011. If you're wondering what happened to all of the chapters telling how the community finished the bridge, it's because this book wasn't just about building a bridge. This book was more about love. Not just any kind of love—unconditional love. Love for our God and love for our neighbors. The people in Nicaragua are my neighbors, and I deeply love them.

But even with the bridge being completed and this book at the end, I still had one prayer that had remained unanswered. That prayer was for God to allow me to find my birth mother. If God had only a single blessing waiting for me on the other side of this mountain I had just climbed, in my heart I wanted so bad for this to be it.

Then on Monday, July 18th, as I shared the news with several co-workers about the bridge being completed, I got a phone call from the agency that had been searching over two years for my birth mother . . . they had located and spoken with her! At that moment, it was almost like the Lord was saying, "Thomas, you've been faithful to the cries of MY people . . . and now, here is YOUR blessing."

Later that week, I reflected back on the past two years and everything that had happened in my life. I began to think about where this faith journey had started. It started with me searching and praying for a renewed purpose in my life. Then the vision the Lord gave me. And one day, the fulfillment of that vision . . . *At the age of 60, I died and went to Heaven. I found myself face-to-face with Jesus. Looking into my eyes, He asked me one question, "Twenty years ago, I gave you this vision, and now, who have you helped in the past twenty years?" Thinking back, my eyes quickly fell upon His face; my head raised high as I answered, "The least of these, Lord . . . the least of these."*

The question you may now have is, "Where can I start MY journey?" If you desire to accept Jesus as the Savior and Lord of your life, let me encourage you to pray the following:

Dear Lord Jesus, thank You for loving me. I believe with all my heart that You are the Son of God and that You died on the cross for my sins. I know I have sinned. I ask You to forgive me. I turn away from my life of sin and selfishness and receive You as my Savior and Lord. I want to learn to love You, trust You, and serve You. Thank You for coming into my life. I pray in Your name. Amen.

If you want to rededicate your life to Christ, let me encourage you to pray the following:

Lord Jesus, I acknowledge You afresh as my Savior and Lord. I confess my tendency to wander from You. Draw me back to Yourself with cords of love. Fill me with Your Spirit. Give me the strength of mind and heart I need each day to live for You. Use my life to make a difference in this world for the sake of Your kingdom. I pray in Your name. Amen.

Now begin living out the most important command in the Bible as given by Jesus, *"Love the Lord your God with all your heart, all your soul, and all your mind"* (Matthew 22:37 NCV). Then follow the second command given by Jesus, *"Love your neighbor as you love yourself"* (Matthew 22:39 NCV). Do something as simple as visiting a person in the hospital and taking them a card with ten one-dollar bills inside and a copy of this book, simply to encourage and assure them that God loves them and IS listening to their prayers.

Ask God to show you a mountain; when you see it . . . start climbing. Then, when adversity is hurled your way, don't stop climbing. And no matter what people may say, *never* look back. Most importantly . . . enjoy the climb!

VISION 2012

WILL YOU BE "ONE"?

Is there a need for another bridge? Yes. There are two communities which each need a footbridge so their children can attend school and so they can sell their milk and produce in the nearby town when the river floods during the rainy season. In May of 2011 I introduced "Vision 2012—Will you be 'one'?" to my church, which is 500 people giving $50 each. It's a challenge for my church congregation and other believers to share with others the need for these bridges.

That would raise $25,000. What about the other $25,000? I'm praying for one person who will hear about the need and feel led to fully sponsor the other bridge.

And what if no one does? Then I don't want to be the person who chooses which community has to wait another year for their bridge.

How much money has been given to date? $3020 (as of June 15, 2012). Monthly updates at www.tenonedollarbills.com

What if you don't reach your goal? I have faith in God that the money will be raised. I gave the Matiguas town officials my word that I would be back to build a bridge for another community. I will *not* go back to Nicaragua without the money to build those two bridges.

How can someone make a contribution? People can send a tax deductible contribution marked "Nicaragua Bridge II" to: Sandy Level Baptist Church, P.O. Box 518 Blythewood, SC 29016. Any amount donated would be greatly appreciated. Even the smallest amount will do great things in the hands of the Lord.

What motivates you? The challenges posed by working on a seemingly impossible project, like building the Gavilan-Patastule bridge in Nicaragua, and looking back and seeing how God provided all the answers.

When will the *Vision 2012* book be finished? In 2013, after the money is raised for the bridge materials and the bridges are completed for these two communities. Will *you* be "one" to help finish writing this story?

ABOUT THE AUTHOR

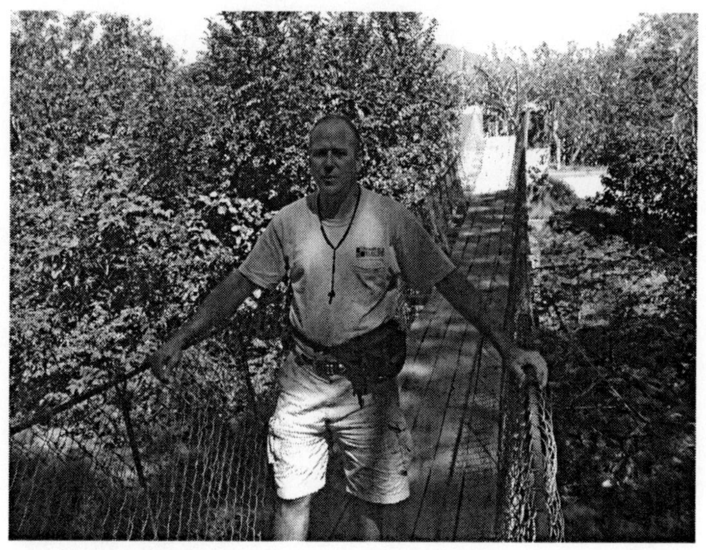

Thomas Black is Vice President of Engineering at Fairfield Electric Cooperative in Blythewood, South Carolina. He is a member and deacon at Sandy Level Baptist Church in Blythewood. He is married to Cynthia, a wonderful wife of eighteen years, and stays busy raising two teenagers, Shelley and Jordan. In 2010, he served as the project coordinator for the Gavilan-Patastule Suspended Bridge near the town of Matiguas in Nicaragua.

Thomas graduated from the University of South Carolina at Lancaster in 1989 with an Associate in Science, and from Clemson University in 1992 with a Bachelor of Science in Electrical Engineering. He is a registered Professional Engineer with the state of South Carolina.

biblesnoopdog IS BORN

Wednesday, September 22nd, 2010 will remain in my memory forever. It was the first Wednesday following The Bridge of Hope car wash fundraiser. Jeannie had called me to share the exciting news that her church had voted to support the Nicaraguan bridge. But as much as I wanted to keep that news to myself, to surprise everyone the next Sunday when I would give the bridge update, I knew I couldn't. I first shared the news with my friends at Bridges to Prosperity—Ken, Avery, Milosz and Robyn, then with Mike and Pastor Ben. I titled the e-mail "It Wasn't Just a Car Wash—Bridge Update."

Thursday night, I got an e-mail from Ken, stating, "I think you need to take these lyrics and modify them to fit YOUR story. This could be a lot of fun." The rest of the e-mail contained the original words to the "Car Wash" song, a popular song and movie from the 1970's. I sent an immediate reply to him, "Ken, I was waiting for another reply from you. You are crazier than I am. I would have never in my life thought of this. I had totally forgotten that song; now it will be in my head all night."

He was up late that night, as his reply back to me near midnight was almost as immediate, "OK . . . just did first two stanzas to give you some ideas." His rendition of the song followed:

Woo-ooo

You might not ever get rich
But let me tell ya it's better that diggin' a ditch.
There ain't no tellin' who ya might meet.
A groovin' pastor or maybe even an angel so sweet.

Come summer the mission work gets kinda hard
This ain't no place to be if ya planned on being a star.
Let me tell you it's always cool
And The Boss don't mind sometimes if ya act a fool.

For some reason, the idea of a song remained in my head that Friday morning. I remembered as a teenager, my friends and I would always try and come up with rap songs. Most, I admit, were really lame. But the thought of those days made me reminisce as I drove my son to school that morning.

Driving, I began to think of words associated with the car wash, thinking of words that would rhyme . . . soap and Bridge of Hope, waxing and relaxing, water and hotter, and drowning and clowning. After dropping Jordan off at middle school, I began to put sentences together, thinking to myself, *This could be fun.* As I pulled into the grocery store shopping center to pick up a few things, I began to type on my phone. I typed the first four stanzas of what would become the car wash rap.

As I hit the send button, my thoughts were, *I'll show him I'm game for this.* Ken's response to this e-mail was surprising, "Yeah!!!" With that type of response, I had to ask the obvious question, "You like it? Written this morning in one typing session . . . sitting in my truck after dropping my son off at school. Not even a rough draft, it just flowed out—hard to explain."

At this point, I wasn't sure what was going on, as Ken sent a message later that evening that stopped me in my tracks, "You have obviously missed your true calling . . . being a Christian rap writer." As his words sank into my heart and I re-read the rap, I felt like this was something I COULD do, so I replied, "LOL I guess I'm a man of many talents. I will not quit my day job. But I will finish the song with the story, and the miracle ending. This is fun. And it will be fun to perform—I'll do it. It will have a great message. And packaged with the bridge story, people will be inspired and their faith will be strengthened. This could be a witnessing tool."

I believe Ken was as excited as me about the rap, as he e-mailed me that night, "We would love it if you recorded the bridge car wash miracle rap and put it on YouTube . . . then we will link to it on our website!" I could feel God calling me to do this, so I replied back, "Yes. I will do it for you Ken and in memory of Orlando." I told Avery I needed to start learning to say "No." I was sure my church youth group would love to do a music video. I had an idea—sports cars, muscle cars, and tricked out trucks. But then, an old lady drives up in an old dirty car with dents . . . and gives the miracle gift. It might work.

I finished the car wash rap that Friday. Saturday morning as I read back over it, I added another verse and took out the last two lines of the song, because that ending was MY idea. I e-mailed Ken the final draft, thanking him for the idea of doing a car wash song. Initially, I had thought this was crazy, but then I realized how this could be a huge outreach—how God showed up when I least expected Him to. Wow!

It Wasn't Just a Car Wash
words inspired, written by Thomas Black

Gotta car wash for th' Bridge of Hope,
So get th' buckets and th' soap.
'Cause down in Nica. people are drownin',
Grab those hoses 'n stop th' clownin'

People gotta cross, th' river is high,
Hope is lost, the bridge is nigh.
Another life's taken, all seems loss,
But we have th' power of th' Cross. (th' power of the Cross)

Gotta wash cars to raise 6 grand
So get your head outta th' sand
'n start washin' 'n waxin',
No time for relaxin', 'cause it's a car wash.

Chorus
Washin' cars, all day long,
Supportin' th' mission, can't go wrong.
Workin' together, workin' as one.
Praisin' God, under th' sun.
Gettin' tired, gettin' hotter,
But gotta save people from th' water.

Here they come, two by two,
Time to get washin', get them thru.
Lookin' for th' miracle yet to be seen,
Hey! Stop doubtin' and you start believin'

Minute by minute th' lines getting longer,
Second by second my faith's getting stronger.
Parking lots full, as cars gettin' cleaner,
Everyone lookin', but no one's seen her.

A miracle will happen it's been foretold,
Ya'll keep washin', young and old,
Washin' 'n sprayin', people are payin',
Day's almost done, so we start prayin'.

A car's pullin' in, crumpled and battered,
Wash it anyways, it shouldn't matter.
Her car's all clean, though it's a wreck,
Rollin' down the window, hands me a check.

We start rejoicin'
Bells start ringin'
Now all can proclaim
In th' power of Jesus name! (th' power of Jesus name!)

The 6 grand was given
Better start believin'
No more drownin'
The bridge is comin'

Chorus
Washin' cars, all day long,
Supportin' th' mission, can't go wrong.
Workin' together, workin' as one.
Praisin' God, and th' Son.
Gettin' tired, gettin' hotter,
We're gonna save people from th' water.

This rap is over, th' end of the story
But it's only the beginnin' of God's glory.

I took out the church newsletter story I had written about the little girl losing her flip-flop in the river. Sitting at the computer, I said to myself, "If I'm called to write these rap songs, then I should be able to take this story and write it into a rap too." That night, I finished the second rap, titled, "It Was Only a Flip-Flop."

During Sunday school, after a lady had excitingly shared about a book she was writing, I got up the nerve to tell everyone about the car wash. I stated, "We raised over $500 at the car wash last Saturday, and I've discovered a new spiritual gift." Everyone seemed to get really interested in what I was about the tell them. "I can write rap music." There was silence and looks of "what did he just say" and "what are you talking about." But as I read through the two raps I had written, they all put smiles on their faces. And after I told them the story of the ten one-dollar bills and Jeannie's church, they really smiled.

On Monday, I sat down and began looking through the bridge design manual, reviewing all the details, when a question came into my mind, "I wonder if anyone has ever done a rap song about the bridge construction?" There was a lot of material to work with. And so it was to be, a rap song not only about the bridge construction, but also about Ken's staff and other volunteers. I actually finished the "B2P" and "Bridge of Hope" raps that week, and was later given the nickname by Ken of "Bible Snoop Dog."

Then the idea popped in my head: why not create a picture slide show which would have pictures to go with the rap? I shared with Robyn at B2P my idea, and she loved it, and sent me over fifty pictures to look through. After looking through them, I realized the rap had information voids, so I wrote some additional rap lines to include those details. After another week, the slide show was finished. But now, who was going to record the rap? I admit, I enjoy singing in the church choir and performing solos, but I was not a rapper. But, as it turned out, I did in fact record the rap.

I got out an old electronic keyboard, one I had paid three dollars for at a church yard sale years ago. This was my "beat box." All the tools I needed to turn all these pieces into a YouTube video, including the software, I already owned. What surprised me even more was when I overlaid the recorded audio on the video slide show, it was only off by one second—something I easily fixed. As I played the entire video, I was even more amazed that the slide transition timing with the audio was perfect the very first time, for every slide!

Since recording the "B2P" and "Bridge of Hope" rap last year, I've written, recorded and created other YouTube rap videos, such as: "We All Need Help," "It Was Only a Flip-Flop," "Killer Bees," and "Third World Countries." Other raps I've written but not yet recorded include: "It Wasn't Just a Car Wash," "Sunday Morning," and "My Story."

I know you may be asking why I haven't recorded a video for the car wash rap. It's because I want that rap video to be the best one, even professionally done. I get emotional just reading the title of the rap "It Wasn't Just a Car Wash," not only because of the miracle gift given as a result, but because a Christian rapper, biblesnoopdog, was born from it.

CPSIA information can be obtained at www.ICGtesting.com
Printed in the USA
LVOW06s1039150415

434564LV00002B/3/P